Walking in God's Glory Realm

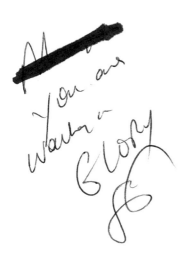

OTHER BOOKS BY SHERLOCK BALLY:

DEALING WITH
THE STORMS OF LIFE

ENDUED AND MANTLED

FROM TRIALS TO TRIUMPH

WORSHIP—WHEN
GOD WALKS AMONG US

PSALMS 102 AND
THE LAST DAYS PROPHECIES

GLORY—WHERE
ATMOSPHERES COLLIDE

WALKING IN GOD'S GLORY REALM

By
Dr. Sherlock Bally

Published by:
Susan K. Reidel
Logos to Rhema Publishing
sreidel@hotmail.com
(918) 606-5346

Unless otherwise noted, all Scripture taken from

THE KING JAMES VERSION

ISBN -10#
ISBN -13#

*Published in the
United States of America by*

Susan K. Reidel
Logos to Rhema Publishing
sreidel@hotmail.com
(918) 606-5346

*Interior design and typography
Roger D. Smith*

Printed in the United States of America

CONTENTS

Chapter 1

THE LORD'S PRAYER: ANSWERS FROM HEAVEN

John 17:20-26 states: *"20 Neither pray I for these alone, but for them also which shall believe on me through their word;*

21 That they all may be one; as thou, Father, art in me, and I in thee, that they also may be one in us: that the world may believe that thou hast sent me. 22 And the glory which thou gavest me I have given them; that they may be one, even as we are one: 23 I in them, and thou in me, that they may be made perfect in one; and that the world may know that thou hast sent me, and hast loved them, as thou hast

*loved me. ²⁴ Father, I will that they also,
whom thou hast given me, be with me
where I am; that they may behold my
glory, which thou hast given me: for thou
lovedst me before the foundation of the
world. ²⁵ O righteous Father, the world
hath not known thee: but I have known
thee, and these have known that thou
hast sent me. ²⁶ And I have declared unto
them thy name, and will declare it: that
the love wherewith thou hast loved me
may be in them, and I in them."*

It is common practice for people, when they
are in a time of need or challenge, to call the
intercessors, the Pastor, or someone to pray.
People who understand warring in the spirit,
warring in the heavenlies are at a spiritual
premium and I do not mean people who can
pray a peripheral prayer. I mean people who
can exercise authority over the powers of the
enemy. People who can confront the enemy
and deal with these situations because they
know who they are in Christ. It is a wonderful
thing when two or three can agree on earth as

touching anything. What an enormously powerful trichotomy. Firstly they agree, secondly they agree on earth, and thirdly the situation is touched.

I have found it to be a reviving moment when I find people of this spiritual caliber and calling. But even though these people are there, even though they are few and far apart, they still have to deal with the fleshly, human limitation that is in them. There is a flesh imposed limit on human understanding so we can only see thus far and go thus far. There are areas of life that are so deep that complete understanding is elusive. With all our heart and desire to touch the lives of people, there are times when the needs are so deep, the challenge so profound, that only God is capable of giving the insight for deliverance.

JESUS PRAYS

The prayer of John 17:20-26 is the Lord's prayer. So many see Matthew 6 as the Lord's prayer. However, Matthew 6 was the model prayer for the disciples and was the prayer that they should pray. Now in John 17, we see Jesus Himself praying a prayer for His people. We must pause and consider the eternal enormity of this thought - Jesus, who is God in the flesh, Jesus who indwells me by the power of the Holy Spirit is praying a prayer for His people. He who knows all about the God-head because He is part of it, He who knows the past, present and future, is praying for me. He who knows things about me that are so deep, things that I don't even know, He is praying a prayer for me. He who is infallible and incomparable, He is praying to the Father for me. As powerful as the prayer of the intercessor is, as wonderful as the prayer of the Pastor is, the thought that Jesus has prayed a prayer for you, forces the thought of supernatural breakthrough. This is a fact that must be meditated on and carefully examined. This prayer means that Jesus, who knows what we will face, Jesus who knows the internal and external challenges that we will confront, is bringing a prayer into our lives. I submit that this prayer contains supernatural answers and breakthrough for the people of God. I have been very surprised not to see more literary material dealing with John 17:20-26.

FOR THOSE WHO BELIEVE

I want to examine this prayer and see what relevance it has to what God's people are facing.

John 17:20-26, verse 20 states: "*Neither pray I for these alone, but for them also which shall believe on me through their word;*"

This prayer was prayed for those who shall believe, it was a prayer for the believers. This in itself is a revelation because in this verse He was not praying for the nonbeliever. The impact on the world will be seen later in the prayer but to begin this entire glorious sequence, He starts with the believer. There are some things that will happen through the believer but firstly some things must happen to the believer.

Jesus was talking to His Father on behalf of those who would believe. Let it be known that when I am in a trauma or a trial, if I feel the pangs of defeat or the celebration of victory, in whatever state I am, I believe. Let this thought never leave your heart for it is one of fundamental importance. Jesus is praying for those who believe and you are one of them. The fact that you believe includes you in this prayer. I submit to you and you shall see this in this prayer, that all you need for victory, conquest, development and increase are found here.

UNITY IN A POSITION

Verse 24 states: *"Father, I will that they also, whom thou hast given me, be with me where I am; that they may behold my glory, which thou hast given me: for thou lovedst me before the foundation of the world."*

Here the Bible declares that Jesus is praying about the unity among believers. We know that there is considerable disunity among believers today that is caused by doctrinal disagreement, denominational walls and a host of other things. Jesus is saying that they all may be one as He and the Father are one. This unity is based on and founded in a position that is already established. He prays, just as the Father and I are one, they too can be one in us.

Over 120 times in the Pauline epistles the words, *"IN CHRIST,"* are mentioned. God reiterates the position of the believers in Christ as a reminder of a finished work. I was given this position at the moment of salvation and this becomes the foundation of the unity among believers. The possibility and reality of unity is not based on the condition of complete agreement on every subject but it is based on the position that we all have been given in Christ. As long as you are saved, you are placed into this great position IN CHRIST. Even though we have been placed individually, we are now in this glorious place together. The many satanic attacks to create disunity whether they are doctrines or methods, personal posturing, political positioning, territorial claims or rank rebellion, they are insignificant compared to our glorious position IN CHRIST. Our Lord is praying for this unity to become real among His people.

The next words are *"...that the world may believe that Thou has sent me."* He connects the unity of the believer to the response of the world. It is quite evident that believers and churches have not made the impact on their communities, regions, states and country or the world that they were called to make. Is there any question as to the reason for this state of affairs?

SATAN'S KINGDOM UNITED

Disunity comes, many times because of personal feeling, personal actions, and personal position. This attitude of bigotry and selfishness robs believers of the opportunity to impact the world. We are called to be selfless but many become selfish. We are expected to be united by our position, but many choose to be disunited by preferences. We are called to be servants but many have the attitude of master: we are called to impact our world but many have a negative influence on the world because of visible division. There are some that are making a significant impact on our world but so many have chosen the path of dangerous divisiveness. Regrettably, they are not only divided, many are the promoters of division.

Herod and Pilate were enemies but they came together to crucify Jesus. Iran and Syria were enemies, they have come together to oppose Israel. Russia and China were enemies, they have come together to be expansionists. Between August 28th and September 5th, 1999, about 4000 delegates representing 150 world religions gathered for a centennial celebration. In attendance were Buddhist, Orthodox, Anglican, Catholic, Hindu, Confucian, Native American and various Muslim groups. In addition there were Taoist, The Fellowship of Isis, Covenant of the goddess, Wicans, The Therosophical Society and many more in attendance. This represents a smorgasbord of religions and a buffet of beliefs that showed the strong presence of goddess worshippers, witches and others of like mind. The document that was constructed by those religions was called 'Towards a Global ethic, a critical declaration.' This consisted of a set of rules that all the religions of the world could agree upon. They said it replaced intolerant exclusionary teaching such as those of the Bible. Their beliefs include secular humanism and is the social contract of the New World Order.

The purpose behind this entire movement is to provide a pseudo salvation, a man made spiritual move and a salvation that is earth based. The ultimate purpose is to remove the thought of salvation through Jesus so that a millennial kingdom, without Jesus Christ can be constructed.

Since this time many other meetings of this kind have taken place and these people are well on their way to creating a stew of religions, a collection of beliefs that is mind boggling. Think of the extreme differences in the belief system of these religions, some of them so extreme that reconciliation of all the differences seems impossible. Yet, they have put their differences aside, their bigotries have been disregarded and they have come together to endeavor to replace Jesus and form their own method of salvation. Yes, they are united and here we are, here we stand, with doctrinal squabbles. Here are some Christians, so divided on doctrinal issues that have nothing to do with Heaven, hell, salvation or our core beliefs. Oh God help us!

Astonishingly, most all of these religious groups have no doctrinal similarities yet they came together under one banner and formed this document called 'Towards a global ethic'. Their unity was used to create a document that would have a gigantic impact on a gullible world. A world seeking something that is spiritual was fed this stew of Godless amalgamation. Wow! Enemies can become friends for the greater purpose of impacting the world with their skewed message. Hundreds of religions can come together, transcending religious boundaries, racial boundaries and significant indifferences to take their message to the world. But what about us?

THE CHURCH DIVIDED

And now here is the church, hung up on whether the church is going up before, in the middle or after the tribulation period; hung up on whether the gifts of the Spirit are for today; separating themselves from one another, aggressively pursuing disunity because of indifference. In the midst of this self-imposed, self-promoting and self-perpetuating disunity, how dare we complain about not touching the world?

So I return to my original text in John 17 where, there are so many important elements covered, that it would take volumes to examine them all. My aim is to zero in on the points of this prayer that have to do with glory. However, I feel spiritually compelled to deal, at least somewhat, with some other details of this prayer.

The absolute first verse, the first words of this prayer center around the unity of the believer in the God given position of being in Christ and its connection to touching the world. We have seen enemies come together to further their mission and lead the world into deception. Religions have sacrificed their beliefs on the altar of unity to come together to deceive an on-looking world. Whether they are new age, nominally Christian, witches, they came together. So I ask, "Does the devil's kingdom have more unity than the church? Does the church that we see have more disunity than the kingdom of darkness? Is the kingdom of Satan united in its purpose and mission?" This demands a spiritual response.

Put aside your territorial claims to that which God owns. Cast aside your personal kingdom building policies where you protect your little kingdom. Violently remove anything that will create and perpetuate disunity. Discard your political posturing to recruit personal support. This is the kingdom of God, not the domain of man. This is the move to touch the world, not protect your little world surrounding your life. You will soon stand before an awesome God who will ask you to give account of your stewardship. You see, sir or madam, you were never, never the owner, you were only the steward. The owner protects his own stuff, the steward is accountable to Almighty God.

I had to write these few words on this point even though my emphasis is on the Glory of God. I have found out that God's interest is the world and all through the Scripture, He touched men and women so that they could touch their nations and the world. He called Israel to be a light to the world. What destiny we forfeit for moments of fleshly satisfaction! What moments of breakthrough and impact we rob ourselves of because of the attitude of pride and selfishness! Flesh, control and self-will have taken charge of so many lives and left in their wake, wrecked spiritual lives and ruined visions and dreams. His prayer began with, "That they may be one even as He and the Father are one."

AND THE GLORY THAT YOU HAVE GIVEN ME

Verse 22 states: "*And the glory which thou gavest me I have given them; that they may be one, even as we are one.*"

I have studied this Holy Bible for over 40 years as of this date, and whenever I read this text, I am always moved by the impact of these words. He is praying to the Father saying, *"The Glory that You have given Me, I have given to them"*. Almighty God has given glory to Jesus. This reflects the oneness in the Godhead in that Jesus, even though He is God, receives from the Father. I call this voluntary subjection without affecting divine attributes. This glory that God the Father gave to God the Son is now given to His people. 13 times in these 6 verses the words *they, them, these* are used. The frequency with which Jesus refers to us who are His, shows His absolute love for us. Glory as God knows it, Glory as heaven knows it, Glory so pure and powerful has been given to us. It is not that this Glory is being given, or it shall be given. The Bible states that it has been given. It is an accomplished fact, so here is the big question. If Jesus has already given this Glory to His children then where is it?

GLORY GIVEN—WHERE IS IT?

Glory comes from God's heaven, from God's dimension, from God's eternity. Discouragement, depression, despair come from earth's dimension which is time. Satan is the prince of the air which is the atmosphere in the world. This entire world as a system and a spirit lies in wickedness and the force of the enemy comes against the believer from 3 positions. The attack comes from the world, the flesh and the devil. The attempt is to create a mess in every department of life. Jesus gives glory and Satan gives a mess. When I did not know the Lord, my entire life was infected and surrounded by mess and messy situations. I want to suggest that the opposite of glory, is mess.

So here is the big question. If glory has been given to me, and it is an accomplished fact, where is it? When you look at Christians generally, do you see more glory or more mess? Why are so many Christians governed by mess and messy situations? This is a question that must be addressed and answered. I used to be in darkness, governed by mess, surrounded by messy situations and acted like it at times. Now I am a temple, created to be filled with the Glory of God, yet still so many have allowed mess to be more dominant in their lives than Glory. If I had no glory when I lived in the messy situation of an un-regenerated life, why should I allow mess to be dominant in my temple?

So many who are saved are dominated by depression, oppression, anxiety, panic, fear, lust, strongholds and fortresses. All of this is allowed to come in to the temple that God has created to house His Glory. What a magnificent honor was bestowed on us when Almighty God chose to give His glory to His Son to be given to us. I was not made a temple to house the messy stuff of my past life. In my past life I was an unrepentant deliberate sinner and that is what I did. I was a sinner so I sinned and I housed the mess that sin brought. When I was that, (a sinner), I housed this (the mess) and my actions were governed by that. Now I have become a temple, I should no longer house the mess and have my actions governed by this.

Where did we lose the message, the revelation of being the temple to be filled

with His Glory? This should be easy to understand because the tabernacle of the Old Testament was built to be filled with the Glory of God. We will deal with this in detail in another chapter. If the Old Testament tabernacle was filled with Glory, why is it difficult for Christians to grasp that the New Testament temple will be filled with God's Glory? You are the temple of the Holy Ghost. In this short prayer of 6 verses, the Glory of God is mentioned twice. Why isn't this Glory that has already been given more visible in the lives of God's people?

Chapter 2

GLORY—GOD'S REALM

When you speak about the Glory of God to God's people, they seem to have very little or no means to grasp the depth of this reality. They immediately begin to think of predictable manifestations and they equate that to the Glory of God. This is not a proper perception of the Glory of God. Remember that Jesus mentioned the Glory of God twice in this short prayer which indicates the primary importance of the Glory of God to the believer.

Jesus, who knows your past, present and future, who knows things about you that you don't know about yourself, prayed that you would receive Glory. This in itself is an astonishing thought. He knows our weaknesses, infirmities, struggles and still speaks of us knowing the Glory of God twice in this prayer. Think with me for a moment. When Christians pray, the major part of the prayer time concerns healing, blessing, deliverance, family, resources and many other things. These things must be prayed about but I find it interesting that Jesus did not mention any of these things in His prayer. However, He does mention Glory twice. It now raises the question, Why? Why did Jesus not pray for the things that we normally pray for when those things are legitimate? He zeroed in on the Glory of God. Let us examine this carefully.

John 1:1,14 states: "*1 In the beginning was the Word, and the Word was with God, and the Word was God. 14 And the Word was made flesh, and dwelt among us, (and we beheld His Glory, the Glory as of the only begotten of the Father,) full of grace and truth.*"

Verse 14 presents some astonishing revelation in relation to the dwelling, the beholding and the glory. The verse states that we behold His Glory full of grace and truth. If grace and truth are parts of Glory, then grace and truth are not Glory. They are only a small part of Glory for Glory is the realm or dimension in which grace and truth reside.

Philippians 4:19 states: *"¹⁹ But my God shall supply all your need according to his riches in glory by Christ Jesus."*

My God shall supply all my needs according to His riches in Glory. Riches cannot be Glory. It is only a part of Glory. This Glory which is the realm of God or the dimension of God is the sum total of all that God has in store for us. By saying that He gave us Glory, He is saying that He is offering us the realm or dimension in which all that we need resides.

Revelation 21:23 states: *"And the city had no need of the sun, neither the moon, to shine in it: for the glory of God did lighten it, and the Lamb is the light thereof."*

The healing, deliverance, joy, praise, power, supply, resource, they all reside in this realm. He has given us all in one realm, the realm of His Glory.

MANIFESTATION OR REALM

To equate the Glory of God to a mere manifestation of Glory, is to actually minimize the enormity of Glory, to minimize not the essence of Glory but to expose a misperception of Glory. Glory produces manifestations but at its essence, is much more than this. I feel that this manifestation craze has been a subtle detour to get people derailed from the true nature and impact of Glory. If it is a manifestation as some espouse, then it is spasmodic and has minimal impact. It will only happen in certain places at certain times, BUT if it is a dimension or realm, we can walk in it, take it home, or to the job or the store. It becomes a realm in which we can live, not just something that we have at times.

Think on this for a moment. What realm do you live in? What things surround your life? Do we feel that God will deliver us internally and leave us to be battered and beaten externally? It does not mean that you won't have trouble, but it means that trouble won't have you. It does not mean that you won't be attacked by the enemy but it means that 'attack' will not dominate your life. Living in God's Glory realm does not mean the absence of attack but the assurance of victory. When you speak of walking in the dimension of Glory or the realm of Glory, people make this the equivalent of weirdness, and peculiarity. This is a gross misunderstanding.

LIFE FROM ANOTHER WORLD

We are in the world but not of the world. This means that even though we walk on earth we are not framed by the world's systems and power.

Hebrews 6:4, 5 states: *4 "For it is impossible for those who were once enlightened, and have tasted of the heavenly gift, and were made partakers of the Holy Ghost, 5 And have tasted the good word of God, and the powers of the world to come."*

We taste the powers of the world to come which means before your body gets to Heaven, Heaven gets to your body.

Matthew 6:10 states: *"Thy kingdom come, Thy will be done in earth, as it is in heaven."*

It is God's will for His kingdom to come to you and His will should be executed as easily as it is in heaven.

Luke 12:32 states: *"Fear not, little flock; for it is your Father's good pleasure to give you the kingdom."*

It is the good pleasure of the Father to give you His kingdom. Yes it is other worldly, life, glory, power from another world. It cannot be that Almighty God has the power to deliver you from the power of darkness, put you in the kingdom of light and then leave you to be beaten by the elements of the kingdom you were delivered from. Beaten enemies should not have domination over me!

God speaks to us in this text in Hebrews and connects our inheritance to light and then speaks of our translation into another kingdom. So we are delivered from the "Power" of darkness and translated into the kingdom of His dear Son according to Colossians 1:13. Wow! The power of darkness has no hold on me internally or externally and now I have the blessing of the kingdom of His dear Son. I will deal with the issue of the Glory of God and light in another chapter but here is this text in Colossians 1:13. I am taken out of the powers of darkness or the realm of darkness and I am put into the Kingdom of His dear Son. I am literally, at the point of salvation taken out of one realm and put into another.

When you look at Israel, as long as they were rightly related to the Ark, with their worship and obedience, no enemy would stand against them. They walked in a realm that was supernatural where even their shoes never wore out. Do you have any idea how much meat, or drink it took to satisfy 3 million people? As long as they followed the cloud, their supply was with them. They literally walked in a different realm. Yes, they were walking through a wilderness but all that they needed was miraculously supplied. I am not suggesting that you will walk around in a bubble, but wherever you walk, you shall be protected. I am not saying that you will walk around with a halo around you, but the light of God will be upon you.

BUYING INTO THE LIE

Where did we buy into the deception that we would walk in the realm of defeat, despair, discouragement and disdain. This thought is not of God, yet it is the realm or the reality that has framed many lives. Many have made this defeat and discouragement their method of operation and this is the realm they live in.

Sadly, they are still held by the power of darkness even though Jesus delivered them from it.

The glory Jesus is speaking of is much more than an off and on, spastic experience. God's will is that we walk in the light as He is in the light.

1 John 1:6, 7 states: *"⁶If we say that we have fellowship with him, and walk in darkness, we lie, and do not the truth:*

⁷But if we walk in the light, as he is in the light, we have fellowship one with another, and the blood of Jesus Christ his Son cleanseth us from all sin."

I must repeat Colossians 1:13. He has delivered us from the power of darkness. The Greek word for power is 'sphere'. This is a powerful statement. We have been delivered from the realm or sphere of darkness. Why should you go back to walking in the realm or sphere when you were delivered from it? The Greek translation of darkness says, "blindness, misery, hatred." Why walk in the blindness so you cannot see the things of God? Why walk in misery when you are destined for the miraculous? Why walk in hatred when the love of God is in you? Yes, God is not only after your inner man but your outer man. He is after your sphere and He wants you to walk in His realm, with His rewards, with His benefits. Out of one realm and into the other, so I am in the world, not of the world.

THE TWO-FOLD CHALLENGE

Romans 6:1; Romans 7:5; Romans 8: 8,9,13 state:

*"**6:1** What shall we say then? Shall we continue in sin, that grace may abound?*

***7:5** For when we were in the flesh, the motions of sins, which were by the law, did work in our members to bring forth fruit unto death.*

***8:8,9,13** ⁸ So then they that are in the flesh cannot please God. ⁹ But ye are not in the flesh, but in the Spirit, if so be that the Spirit of God dwell in you. Now if any man have not the Spirit of Christ, he is* *none of his.* [13] *For if ye live after the flesh, ye shall die: but if ye through the Spirit do mortify the deeds of the body, ye shall live."*

These scriptures individually and collectively give us a powerful revelation that seems to have been partially overlooked by many of God's people. The frequency of its mention indicates the importance that God gives to this revelation. Scriptures that say, shall continue IN SIN, or do not live IN THE FLESH or fulfill not the LUSTS OF THE FLESH, or do not walk IN THE FLESH, and so many more, speak of walking in a realm, or sphere.

According to the word of God, sin is in me because I was born in sin and shaped in iniquity. I have an internal connection with the first Adam because I inherited the Adamic nature. It is the nature of sin that is always inclined to sin. Paul speaks in detail of this internal struggle and we will deal with this in a later chapter. But this is not where the attacks or the attempts of the enemy stop. I also have an external challenge where the Bible says I am in sin. This means, around me there is a realm, or a sphere, of sin. It is here in this external, circumstantial realm that the enemy does all he can to saturate the things around me with his devilish purposes and his diabolical nature.

It is easy to see the world as a place, as a system saturated with evil, as a spirit that is seductive and tempting, striving to dominate the believer. This realm is constantly attacking and opposing the believer because it represents a realm or a sphere that is totally opposed to God. It is opposed to the Godly purposes that God has for us. As you look at the world, you see the devastation of morals, the emotional dysfunction, the societal chaos, the renegade expression of vice and habit. Biblical moral standards are replaced by humanistic values and there is no bridle on rebellious expression. This force of the enemy is constantly bombarding the believer, endeavoring to grind him or her into submission.

If we are conditioned to believe that the normal Christian life, is to be constantly oppressed, controlled, and saturated with this wicked realm, then our battle is lost. God would never plan this for His children's lives.

He sent His Son to die for us and it was not just so that our inner man could be touched.

Along with the revelation of salvation for the inner man, there is thought of being delivered from Satan's attack. Would Jesus die to deliver me in my inner man and then leave me to be pulverized by the attacks of the enemy externally? God delivered the children of Israel from the presence of Pharaoh by the shedding of blood but He delivered them from the power of Pharaoh by drowning the enemy in the Red Sea. The enemies that pursued, the attackers that would not give up, the power of the past had to be dealt with. I am saying to you that we have not taught people with specificity that they do not have to walk in defeat. Discouragement, depression, despair, deterioration are the realm in which so many live. It is doubly defeating when they feel that that is the normal life. Some, thankfully though, have found that this life, while we are on earth can be a life of purpose, power and provision. This life that God has planned for us, this realm that He has provided can be seen so clearly. The phrases IN CHRIST all through the Pauline epistles, WALK IN THE SPIRIT, are some of the keys that unlock the understanding to the realm that God has provided for you.

DOUBLE JEOPARDY— DOUBLE TRIUMPH

According to the Word of God, sin was in me and I was in sin. In me, sin became the power over my emotions: when I was in sin, it became the realm in which I lived and the sphere of my operation. In this sphere, I experienced emotional dysfunction and mental attack where the thoughts of my mind were renegade. I walked in a maze, a fog, and this external walk was my day to day reality. The scripture that states I am in the world but not of the world presents a startling truth, though. Even though my body is in the world, the power of the world should have no control over my life because I am walking in a different realm. Sin in me is my spiritual condition, me in sin is the external realm where I lived but now I have had a magnificent double deliverance. Christ is now in me and I am now in Christ. Christ in me takes care of the 'sin in me' condition.

Many have stressed the internal deliverance and this is preeminently important. But this deliverance internally is also the indicator that there will be a deliverance externally. I am not saying that your walk will be without attack or incident but I am saying that the realm of sin and flesh will have no power to dominate and rule your life. The norm should not be depression and despair, your method of operation should not be hopelessness and discouragement. Why is it so easy to believe that Almighty God has the power to heal, deliver and cleanse us on the inside but the outward realm remains polluted and contaminated? I believe that Paul received an astonishing revelation on this and that is why the words, 'IN CHRIST' are mentioned over 100 times in his epistles.

THREE ATTACKS IN THE WORLD'S LUST OF THE FLESH SPHERE

The lust of the flesh, the lust of the eyes and the pride of life constitute the realm of the world.

1 John 2:15,16,17 states: "*15 Love not the world, neither the things that are in the world. If any man love the world, the love of the Father is not in him. 16 For all that is in the world, the lust of the flesh, and the lust of the eyes, and the pride of life, is not of the Father, but is of the world. 17 And the world passeth away, and the lust thereof: but he that doeth the will of God abideth forever.*"

This world is saturated with these 3 elements that become the 3 methods of attack on the life of the believer. This is not a book to deal with the lethal nature of these attacks or to show how many have opened their lives to this damnable, hell sent, devil inspired trilogy, a sphere, a realm, with 3 satanic thrones to be established in the lives of men and 3 attacks to deal with body, soul and spirit.

THE LUST OF THE FLESH

The lust of the flesh deals with bodily physical appetites, the least of which is food consumption. This lust of the flesh has to do with renegade passion that causes you to love what you should hate and hate what you should love. This first attack is the attack that renders the body bound and subjected to this evil. This has led to a world of evil explosions: teenage pregnancy, abortion, pornography, adultery, fornication and the ominous presence of divorce. Broken lives, broken relationships, broken marriages, and broken homes are left in its wake. What a price to pay for a moment of satanically, fleshly inspired indulgence.

THE LUST OF THE EYES

The lust of the eyes is the runaway desire to see, to have and to possess. The enemy will be sure to open up the appetite to possess because it becomes a bottomless pit that puts people in a free fall. It is the attempt of the enemy to take the eyes of God's people away from Christ and His kingdom. It is the attack to get people to focus on the visible, and be overwhelmed with the cares of life. It is here that Christians become entangled with the affairs of life. Their time is dispensed and apportioned by their priorities so that the cares of life command the greatest portion of their allegiances. I am not speaking of the time spent in the workplace but the free time that is negotiable where we find time to do the things that are important to us. Remember priorities decide pursuit. The lust of the eyes, the desire to possess, the drive to get, when these are renegade and uncontrolled, initiates disaster. The current debt crisis is an accurate reflection of the lust of the eyes in destructive motion. Walking in this realm of the lust of the eyes is an attack on the soul as it contrives ways to stop the inner man from conforming to Christ. It provides another image for your life to then conform to.

In the book of Daniel you read of an image that was made so that people would bow to worship. Even though the king commanded the people to worship, to reinforce this point of worship, to make this fake worship even more forceful and powerful, he had an image built. Now they could see the concrete reality of the call to worship, as they could see what they would be worshipping. The image gave physical form to a spiritual demand and deception. The worship was initially demanded and commanded but now the image gave substance to the false worship. They saw, they chose, they bowed. Of course, there were some that didn't bow, that could not surrender their worship of the true God. This idea of images to create submission is all over the Old Testament. Certain false gods were associated with certain images.

There are two that are outstanding, one in the Old Testament and one in the New Testament. There is the image that Daniel dreamt that symbolized the emperor that would come against Israel but also represented the spirits that were behind these empires that would be revealed in the latter days.

There is another image in the book of Revelation where an image is built to the Antichrist, placed in the temple and worship to him is demanded. If this worship is not given, people that refuse to worship are beheaded.

The building of an image is a vital part of the devil's attempt to get your worship. The world with all its reputations, its glamour, its physical attractiveness, its pleasure creates an image that you can see. It is the devil's attempt to cause you to submit to fake worship. It is the attempt of the enemy to cause you to be controlled by the world. You, though, must have things without them having you. We are speaking of the realm that the world, the flesh and the devil have formed to cause you to walk in. All that this brings is chaos and confusion all around.

THE PRIDE OF LIFE

Now here comes the third element of this satanic realm or sphere, the pride of life. The pride of life has to do with a position of Godless assumption. This is where people do all they can to get into a position of advantage and elevation. It is the assumption that you can use any means to get to the place you want to be. If this involves deception, control, using others, it matters not. The pride of life would be the equivalent of the statement in Genesis that you would be as a god. If you eat this, you shall be as a god. There will be no absolutes that govern your life and no accountability for actions. You will become your own little, frail, puerile god. It would be the equivalent of the devil talking to Jesus and saying that He could cast himself down and angels would take charge. Use His divine power to achieve an earthly position. What an assumption!

These three well organized satanic attacks, the lust of the flesh, the lust of the eyes and the pride of life have brought society to the brink of spiritual, emotional and social disaster.

Every aspect of life has been saturated with this move of Satan to conquer and contaminate. It effects are seen in every area of life and only the touch of Almighty God can extricate men and women from this well woven web of evil.

Chapter 3

THE LUCIFERIC ASSUMPTION

Yes, these are the satanic words. Do what you want, when you want, how you want and your position in Christ will cover you and recover all.

The pride of life is the purposeful, deliberate elevation of self above God, so that the age old desire to be a little god is realized. This possibly is the most subtle and seductive deception of all. How many do you know in the church are driven by the desire to have a position and they will speak, act, perform, or do whatever is necessary to get that position. Words of criticism, destruction, and divisiveness are spoken, hurting those that surround them, but other lives do not matter.

In the midst of God's house, some operate with the same Luciferic motif as Lucifer did in Isaiah 14:12-15: *"12 How art thou fallen from heaven, O Lucifer, son of the morning! how art thou cut down to the ground, which didst weaken the nations! 13 For thou hast said in thine heart, I will ascend into heaven, I will exalt my throne above the stars of God: I will sit also upon the mount of the congregation, in the sides of the north: 14 I will ascend above the heights of the clouds; I will be like the most High. 15 Yet thou shalt be brought down to hell, to the sides of the pit."*

Five 'I wills' culminated in a descent into hell. The fifth 'I will' was that Lucifer would ascend above the heights of the clouds, and he would be like the Most High.

The clouds are always a symbol of the Glory of God and the devil wants to be above this.

Then, he will be the object of glory not God. If only Christians could learn that living the 'I will' life will eventually lead to stealing the Glory of God, maybe, their self-willed, sinister actions would stop. The Luciferic assumption was that if he took this position of ascendancy, he would be like the Most High and this is the most dangerous position of all. This is the same assumption that caused Eve to succumb and it carries a subtle world of deception. It removes the need for submitting to the Almighty absolute God and now you become your own god. There is no need for accountability so life now revolves around you and the 'I will' life becomes your norm. There are so many that are trapped in this unholy vortex of self and addiction to the 'I will' life. This is seen in the home where husbands and wives in many cases live for themselves. Giving and sacrificing are not a part of their lifestyles and the results are seen in broken homes.

This is seen in children who have learned well from what they have seen and in addition, they also carry this addiction to 'I will'. The results are rebellion to authority and no sense of accountability. This is seen in the world, in every sector in the world, in every sector of society, wherever chaos is seen the reality is that there is a lack of accountability and submission. The word submission has now been redefined as a word that has bad connotations. Yes, from Genesis to today, the story has not changed. The pride of life, subtly cloaks the flesh and self with a touch of religious bigotry and says, I will, I will, I will.

SIN CHRONICALLY AND GRACE WILL COVER IT?

The assumption that you can habitually and chronically sin and rebel against God and the grace of God will continue to cover this is a godless assumption and Holy Scripture does not teach this.

Romans 6:1 states *"⁶ What shall we say then? Shall we continue in sin, that grace may abound?"* GOD FORBID! Romans 7:14-22 states, *"¹⁴ For we know that the law is spiritual: but I am carnal, sold* *under sin. ¹⁵ For that which I do I allow not: for what I would, that do I not; but what I hate, that do I. ¹⁶ If then I do that which I would not, I consent unto the law that it is good. ¹⁷ Now then it is no more I that do it, but sin that dwelleth in me. ¹⁸ For I know that in me (that is, in my flesh,) dwelleth no good thing: for to will is present with me; but how to perform that which is good I find not. ¹⁹ For the good that I would I do not: but the evil which I would not, that I do. ²⁰ Now if I do that I would not, it is no more I that do it, but sin that dwelleth in me. ²¹ I find then a law, that, when I would do good, evil is present with me. ²² For I delight in the law of God after the inward man:"*

This Scripture reveals the presence of flesh domination that brings captivity and death that must be dealt with. This is the experience of Paul who gave us most of the New Testament.

Romans 8:6-9 states: *"6 For to be carnally minded is death; but to be spiritually minded is life and peace. 7 Because the carnal mind is enmity against God: for it is not subject to the law of God, neither indeed can be. 8 So then they that are in the flesh cannot please God. 9 But ye are not in the flesh, but in the Spirit, if so be that the Spirit of God dwell in you. Now if any man have not the Spirit of Christ, he is none of his."*

The fleshly mind cannot please God and is at enmity with God.

The sphere of darkness, the sphere of the world is not the sphere that Almighty God wants to dominate me. This is not the sphere He wants me to walk in. You have heard of the Glory realm. This is not just what God has waiting for me in Heaven but something that He has already given to us on earth. Again, people have equated the Glory realm to a realm of manifestations and sometimes pretty strange manifestations. The Almighty is able to do whatever He chooses, this I know. However, it has completely eluded some that the Glory realm really is a realm, a sphere in which we can walk and live, something that should be perpetuated and not be spasmodic.

Paul in Romans 8, is dealing with his internal struggle, his disdain for fleshly operation and his emergence into the walk in the Spirit of Romans 8. Remember that the world is the external enemy and the flesh is the internal enemy. That which is external has no power over me if that which is internal does not endorse and entertain the temptations of the world.

The world as a system and a place is fueled with wickedness.

1 John 4:14 states: *"Beloved, believe not every spirit, but try the spirits whether they are of God: because many false prophets are gone out into the world.*

2 Hereby know ye the Spirit of God: Every spirit that confesseth that Jesus Christ is come in the flesh is of God: 3 And every spirit that confesseth not that Jesus Christ

*is come in the flesh is not of God: and this
is that spirit of antichrist, whereof ye have
heard that it should come; and even now*

*already is it in the world. [4] Ye are of God,
little children, and have overcome them:
because greater is he that is in you, than
he that is in the world."*

The world is saturated with the spirit of the Antichrist and this world becomes the external enemy.

The flesh which is internally centered is also a formidable enemy. This internal enemy is my flesh nature, my connection with Adam. It is that sinful nature that is always inclined to sin and evil. It is the Trojan Horse that is filled with all types of evil potential within my life. When the world offers its seductions, it is only when this internal enemy, the flesh, reaches out and grabs a hold of this, it is only then that the world and its temptations can successfully affect me. Paul, with all his revelation and wisdom, also had to deal with this flesh enemy.

I will show you that the prayer of John 17 covers an internal touch of Glory and an external walk in this Glory realm.

Chapter 4

GLORY IS GIVEN BUT GLORY IS NOT RECEIVED

I have been talking about the two dimensional challenge, sin in you and you in sin. I have further stated that there is a two dimensional blessing, Christ in you and you in Christ. If I have an internal struggle according to Romans 7:14-22 and Galatians 5:17, then there must be an internal answer. If I have an external challenge of walking in the sphere, or under the domination and control of the realm of the world, then I must have an external answer. I dealt with a little of this in a previous book but I must devote some detail to this now.

Glory was given by our Lord in John 17, so why then do we not see that glory displayed more in the lives of people. Why do we see more defeat than victory, discouragement than encouragement, weakness than strength, and more sorrow than joy? Why are there so many that lack vision, lack determination and have such a lack of victorious testimony? The Glory of God, the sum total of all that God wills for us, has already been given to us. It should be elementary now to see evidence of this in the lives of people. Note that the lack of evidence does not negate the fact that this Glory has been given to God's people.

WHERE IS THE DISCONNECT?

So many have found themselves attached to and connected to the despair, hopelessness, defeat and negative ness that characterized their past. Even though they have been gloriously saved, they have become trapped by "stuff". This is why the children of Israel, when they were walking through the Red Sea, walked on dry ground not through mud and mire. God had the power to deliver them from the most powerful sin and had the power to deliver them from the most powerful army. He then opened a gaping pathway in this sea for about three million people. Wow! What would have happened if they were delivered from the enormity of all of that and then were trapped in the sea by muddy residue? So many in church life testify of being wonderfully saved and then are pitifully trapped by residue. Think about the raising of Lazarus and the heavenly quality of this astonishing miracle. Here is a man who was dead and decomposing after four days. His spirit was already in Paradise but the word of Jesus pierced through time into eternity and brought him out. Yet with all this resurrection life, pulsating through his body, when he came out he was bound. He was wrapped in linen clothes and grave clothes, and had to be loosed. Filled with life and bound by grave clothes. The word to the Christian today is, "Be freed from the wrapping, and the grave clothes."

THE CHALLENGE OF GIVING OR RECEIVING

If this Glory is given, why is it not seen? I submit that there is a challenge and a disconnect on the receiving end. It is not that this Glory has not been given, it is that it has not been received. Something has been erected; something has stood in the way of receiving this wonderful offer of the Glory of God. Why would someone who has been offered a supernatural gift, and a Godly realm to walk in, why would they not desire to receive it? Why would they not do all that they can to eliminate any obstacle or hindrance that would stop them from receiving.

Could it be that many are praying for something that has already been given? If so, the more correct prayer is not the prayer for the gift but the prayer should be, 'Lord, eliminate everything that would hinder me from receiving.'

THE NATURE OF THE BEAST

This beastly hinderer that dares to obstruct me from receiving must be identified, targeted and dealt with. This unholy imposter that dares to be a perpetual presence must be brought to naught. What is it? Who is he? How can I deal with it?

When you study the tabernacle of the Old Testament you follow a divine sequence that leads you ultimately to the Glory of God. Let us examine further. As you entered the tabernacle, you came to the outer court where there was the brazen (brass) altar and brazen (brass) laver. The brass indicated judgment and the altar was the place where the blood was shed. The laver was the place of washing with water. May I suggest that the brazen altar took care of the internal - for the internal sin there was the blood, and the external the washing of water. The brazen laver took care of the external because as the priest walked to the temple, he would be touched by the dirt and uncleanliness of the outside. So he washed in the brazen laver before entering the tabernacle to engage in his priestly duties.

At the brazen altar, you would readily see the blood of animals because this is where the animal was sacrificed. Next to it was the brazen laver where there was water so the priest could wash himself. Be reminded that on his way to the temple, he would become unclean by walking and being touched by the dirt and elements around him. So here at the brazen laver he would wash and be made clean. I submit that we become internally contaminated by the elements of the world. Here I see the need for a two-fold cleansing, cleansing on the inside and cleansing on the outside. I see the blood of Jesus as the power of the internal cleansing of my sins. I see the word of God as the power for my external cleansing. We become affected at times by the external elements of the world and find that vices, habits, patterns develop. These must be broken, cleansed, removed. I see the brazen altar,- the shedding of blood, and the brazen laver - the washing of water, to be highly illustrative of 2 types of cleansing in the believer.

Hebrews 10:22 states: *"Let us draw near with a true heart in full assurance of faith, having our hearts sprinkled from an evil conscience, and our bodies washed with pure water."*

Ephesians 5:26 states: *"That he might sanctify and cleanse it with the washing of water by the word."*

Here in these scriptures, our bodies are washed with pure water and we experience the washing of regeneration by the Word. Man belongs to two worlds, the material and the spiritual, the visible and the invisible. Because of the fall of Adam and the inception of sin, both worlds came under the domination of sin. Because sin entered, death came so that attacks and oppression come to these two worlds. Because of this, redemption has to apply to both worlds and deliverance must come from these attacks in the two worlds.

The salvation that was provided by God, does not only deal with sin and attacks in the spiritual world, but it also deals with sin and attacks in the physical world. In the sacred sanctum of your inner man, redemption must be experienced. But in the outer world, the redemption and deliverance must also be experienced.

1John 5:8 states: *"And there are three that bear witness in earth, the spirit, and the water, and the blood: and these three agree in one."*

The same spirit that applies the blood of Jesus to the inner man, is the same spirit that applies the water to the body, or the outer man. Here deliverance and cleansing come externally.

Ephesians 5:26 states: *"That he might sanctify and cleanse it with the washing of water by the word."*

John 13:10 states: *"Jesus saith to him, 'he that is washed needth not save to wash his feet but is clean every whit: and ye are clean, but not all.'"*

John 15:3 states: *"Now ye are clean through the word which I have spoken unto you."*

Here the washing of the water and the word are vitally connected. When the priest saw the brazen altar and the brazen laver as he came to the outer court, there was the introduction of a vital teaching for the New Testament. The Spirit, the water and the blood bear witness on earth. The blood is for the inner man, the water is for the outer man and the Holy Spirit is the one who makes these glorious truths, reality. He is the one who applies the power of the blood and the washing of the Word.

Here is a dynamic connection. Hearts are sprinkled from an evil conscience and bodies are washed with pure water. Who shall ascend to the hill of God or stand in His Holy place: he that hath clean hands and a pure heart. It is an astonishing revelation and a testimony to the Glory of Almighty God, that as you entered the Tabernacle, this was the two-fold revelation that would be given.

I reiterate. As the priest entered the Tabernacle, he would come first to the Brazen

Altar where blood was shed, where he would encounter the shedding of blood. I submit that the shedding of this blood would take care of internal sin. Here, in this same outer court, he would encounter the Brazen laver where he would wash himself in the water since, as he walked to the temple, he would become dirty externally because of wind, dirt and external elements. Washing in this laver, would take care of the external contaminants. I submit that this washing by water would take care of external sin.

Be mindful though, that this entire journey that the priest took through the Tabernacle, would ultimately take him to the Holy of Holies but if the initial process described above was not adhered to, he could go no further. No access would be given to the Holy Place where the table of showbread, the lampstand and the altar of incense stood. Only those who were cleansed could go further. Without this cleansing, no access would be given to the Holy of Holies where the Glory of God fell. All of this great provision of God could not be accessed without the shedding of the blood and the washing by water in the laver.

So for our internal sins there is the shedding of the blood, and for the external realm we have the washing of the Word. A double cleansing. Now the cleansed priest could go into the Holy place which brings a revelation that many do not want to consider. Only the cleansed can enter into the Holy Place. This is not a demand for perfection but the provision for a necessary cleansing before we can approach a Holy God.

There are so many Christians today who are beaten and battered by the outer world of temptation and oppression. Vices and habits attach to them like barnacles to an anchor. Attitudes that are common to the world such as anger, bitterness, pride and arrogance, self-will and independence, somehow attach themselves to the believer. There is a certified attack that is intense and constant from the outer world, the material world, on the believer. It is unthinkable that Almighty God will provide deliverance for my heart and my inner man and leave me to be bound and blasted by the outer world. Thank God that there is a twofold deliverance that has been given to us through the salvation that was provided for us.

We are working our way to identify the beast, the enemy that hinders the reception of Glory. Contaminated folk, people who have purposely rejected the provision for cleansing can never get into the Holy Place. The desire to live in purposeful sin, to avoid the spiritual responsibility to be cleansed, are things that constitute unholy lives. Only the cleansed enter the Holy Place.

Here in this place there are 3 important utensils. They are the Table of Shewbread, the Golden Lampstand and the Altar of Incense. They represent experiencing Jesus as our bread, or our sustenance, experiencing the Power of the Holy Spirit as reflected in the Lampstand and following in prayer and worship as evidenced by the Altar of Incense. So we can say that those who refuse to be cleansed, who choose to live in the mess of sin, will not experience these three things. They will not know Jesus as their daily sustenance, not know the power of the Spirit, and not know the power of prayer and worship.

THE JOURNEY TO GLORY

The ultimate aim of this tabernacle journey was to get to the Holy of Holies where the Ark was and the glory fell. The Holy Place which is represented by the number 5 is the place of Grace. As the High Priest continued into the Tabernacle, he would meet: The Brazen Altar, one; The Brazen Laver, two; The Table of Shewbread, three; The Golden Lampstand, four; The Altar of Incense, five. Five is the number of Grace. Just by way of brief explanation, in Christian circles, the number 5 is seen as the number of Grace just as the number 3 is seen as representing divine abundance; the number 4 as representing earth; 6 – the number of man and 7 as the number of perfection. However, the purpose of the tabernacle journey was not to stay at number five, as wonderful and powerful as the place of grace was, but to get to number seven. Seven is the number of perfection and there is where the Glory fell.

Number 7 was where the Ark of the Covenant was. The Ark was the seventh utensil or article in the journey from the outer court to the Holy of Holies. This is where the Glory of God fell and this was the priest's destination. Here, if he entered with sin in his life, he would be a dead priest. God chose this part of the tabernacle to manifest His Glory - in the Holy of Holies.

How spiritually appropriate and how accurate is the calculation of the Almighty. The object of the journey was to move from number five to number seven. In other words, the journey entailed moving from grace to glory. Grace, or number 5, or the Holy Place was an entrance into another place. The priest would have to go to the Holy of Holies and there the Glory of the Lord would fall.

Let me show you the differences between the Holy Place and the Holy of Holies. Remember, the Holy Place was a wonderful place of provision but it was the doorway to a deeper life. In the Holy Place, someone had to bake the bread, put the incense, and fill the lamps, but in the Holy of Holies it was God and God alone. In the Holy Place there were 3 utensils, in the Holy of Holies only 1, the Ark of the Covenant. In the Holy Place, the priest was blessed; in the Holy of Holies where the

Glory of God came, an entire nation was touched. In the prayer of John 17, several times the word "world" is used. God's interest is not giving this Glory to make you glorious but that the world may know. This in John 17 connects with the fact that when the Glory fell in the Holy of Holies, an entire nation was touched. May I say that messy lives cannot impact the world. Fleshly, carnal lives have no power to impact the world for the Glory of God.

WHAT IS BETWEEN FIVE AND SEVEN?

I still have not answered the big question. What is it that hinders men and women from receiving this great heavenly gift of Glory? Between the numbers 5 and 7 is the number 6, and we know that 6 is the number of man. After you leave the Holy place to get to number 7 or get to the Glory of God, you have to pass through number 6. This number 6 was the veil and Paul said repeatedly and clearly, this veil is my flesh.

In the journey from the outer court to the Holy of Holies, the veil was the 6th article or the 6th thing. Frist the brazen altar, second the brazen laver, thirdly the table of shewbread, fourthly the golden lampstand, fifthly the altar of incense and sixthly, the veil. How appropriate are the numerics of the Almighty God. Six, the number of man and here, six is the veil that stands between the Holy Place and the Holy of Holies. This would represent the things that hinder you from moving into the realm of the Glory of God. The thing that hinders is undoubtedly the flesh.

The veil was the thing that stood between number 5 and number 7. This was the erected thing that stood between grace and glory. We know several things about this veil. IT was very tall, enormous and very heavy. The enemy wants you to believe that the fleshly obstacle between you and the Glory of God is so tall, enormous and heavy, that you will never get past it.

Yes, ladies and gentlemen, the enormity and the heaviness of the flesh, the carnal nature, the center of the 'I will' life; the flesh that is an enemy of God that cannot please

God; the flesh that daily wars against anything that has to do with the Holy Spirit; the fleshly attitude, the absorption with self and the violence of the 'I will' life, this is the hinderer, the imposter, the thief. It will masquerade in different forms, assume different cloaks, and conform to every environment. It is seen in Genesis as the raven. When Noah wanted to see if the flood had abated, he sent out the raven. It never came back because you never send a flesh-loving instrument to bring back a spiritual answer. The raven found it easy to rest its feet on a judged earth full of death and decay. So too, this imposter of flesh will rest on the decay and decomposition, it will feast on death and be comfortable in the environment of sin in our lives. It will erect itself enormously and create great heaviness, just like the veil.

Secondly, the veil was very beautiful, filled with bright colors. The flesh will take the form of the attractive, the beautiful, to seduce you with its filthy appeal. It was not the devil that stopped you, or people, or opinion, it was the presence and operation of the flesh. What has stopped so many from receiving this gift of Glory internally and externally? It is the operation of the flesh that is manifested in a multitude of ways.

Galatians 5: 19-21 gives a list of the works of the flesh and shows its method of operation. *"19 Now the works of the flesh are manifest, which are these; Adultery, fornication, uncleanness, lasciviousness, 20 Idolatry, witchcraft, hatred, variance, emulations, wrath, strife, seditions, heresies, 21Envyings, murders, drunkenness, revellings, and such like: of the which I tell you before, as I have also told you in time past, that they which do such things shall not inherit the kingdom of God."*

The greatest hindrance to the reception of the Glory of God is the exaltation of the flesh. The question must be answered, "How much fleshliness is there in many believers today?" How many lives are founded on I will do what I want, when I want, how I want? How many say that they will not submit to the authority of a pastor because he is just a man. They fail to realize that man was given authority by God. How many live in the fleshly grasp of pride and arrogance so that they are like lords not servants? How many have a life that is seen in the church and another seen at home? How many are addicted to lust so their marriages and homes are on the brink of disaster? How many of our teenage Christians are living in chronic rebellion and promiscuity and lustfulness? How many use coarse words of criticism against others because they believe they have the gift of analysis? There are a hundred more questions but the point is clear. "Do you see a world of fleshliness among many Christians"? Giving up glory for mess? Selling the future for the present? This flesh is the enemy that mocks the lives it controls.

PULLING DOWN THE VEIL

If this veil of flesh isn't pulled down, spiritual death will occur for to be fleshly minded is death. If a decision is not made to live in the Spirit, then the lusts of the flesh will assume preeminence. This flesh must be treated as an enemy not a friend, it must be treated as the evil hinderer that it is.

Romans 8:13 states: *"For if ye live after the flesh, ye shall die: but if ye through the Spirit do mortify the deeds of the body, ye shall live."*

Yes through the operation of the Spirit, we, we, we, do mortify the deeds of the body. It is a willful, purposeful, deliberate slaughtering of this enemy. The Glory of God represents all that is holy, powerful and glorious. The flesh represents all that has to do with sin, with the fall of Adam and with the total absorption with self. As quickly as the Glory of God should be accepted, is as quickly that the flesh should be mortified.   How could so many allow something so evil and destructive to take control of their lives and hinder something so wonderful and heavenly?

But here is the wonderful response from Heaven. Deliverance is possible and it has already taken place. The day that Jesus died, the veil was rent asunder so that never again would it physically hinder the reception of God's Glory.

This tearing down, this rending of the veil was done because of the death of Jesus on the cross. The only way that the flesh can be torn down in the life of the believer is by the appropriation of the work of the cross. His death becomes my death, His crucifixion becomes my crucifixion.

Galatians 2:20 states: *"²⁰ I am crucified with Christ: nevertheless I live; yet not I, but Christ liveth in me: and the life which I now live in the flesh I live by the faith of the Son of God, who loved me, and gave himself for me."*

This flesh cannot be pulled down by flesh, or self-effort, or self-resolution. It must be pulled down in your life by the finished work of the cross.

UNDERSTANDING LUCIFER'S PAST

The problem was never on the giving end because Jesus gave us this Glory. It was always on the receiving end. Why has the enemy fought the reception of Glory so violently? Why did he devise every way possible so that people would not walk in this realm? Think on this for a moment. In eternity past, in Isaiah 14: 12-14, Lucifer did all he could to take that glory. He staged a rebellion and that is why when people choose to rebel, they take the same position that Lucifer took. The result - he was kicked out of heaven.

Jesus, though, gave that Glory to His children so that we can have it internally and externally. Every time the devil looks at the believer and sees that we have free access to something he wanted and could not have, he is incensed and angered. Thus the hatred of the believers and the vicious attack on the believer. He knew the magnificence, the sanctity and the splendor of this Glory. This Glory was and is the thing that forms the sphere of Heaven. He knows that when the believer receives the revelation of Glory, no power, temptation or attack will bring the believer under subjugation and submission to the satanic seduction. It means that the believer will be internally and externally free.

He will no longer be controlled by flesh internally nor walk in the realm or sphere of darkness externally. Here, in the midst of Glory, Satan has lost his ability to control and contaminate.

GLORY TURNS THINGS AROUND

Now we become conquerors not the conquered, the binders not the bound, the chasers not the chased. Remember Lucifer had a first hand, up close, long look at the Glory of God in eternity. The device of the flesh that is so subtly fashioned, so religiously cloaked, so varied and versatile, lets you know the lengths the devil will go through to deceive and deter. He desperately wants to keep you from the realm of Glory. In the Old Testament, when the Ark was with the children of Israel, no enemy, no power regardless of the strength of numbers had the ability to overcome them. In the midst of that glory, they were safe.

Since the devil knows the meaning of Glory and the impact of Glory, he will do all he can to stop you from entering into the realm of Glory. The flesh always wants to be exalted and elevated, and the devil will employ any means, present any temptation to satisfy that fleshly desire for elevation. It is that very thing that got him kicked out of heaven and he will influence the same thing in the life of others. This will cause you to be kicked out of the realm of Glory because of the fleshly absorption with flesh. Beware of the temptation to want to be elevated, to usurp authority and to take what is not yours to take. Remember, the choice to want to be elevated got the devil kicked out of Heaven.

I hope this treatment of the hinderer to the reception of the Glory has helped to cultivate in you a disdain for the flesh in all its operations. Treat it like the plague that it is, and do not buy into its cloaking and seduction. Paul wonderfully explained and exposed it, and then showed us how to mortify it. Do not save what God has targeted for destruction. This is your time to receive Glory and walk in His Glory. May your hearts be full and your realm be glorious.

Chapter 5

MOVEMENT TOWARDS GOD

In John 17, Jesus said that His Glory was given to the believer, an act that was completed in the past. He then goes on to make a powerful declaration in verse 24. It says, "I will that they be with me where I am." Jesus is saying to the Father that this is His will. He wants us to be with Him where He is. This is a most powerful point in relation to the Glory of God. There are many times when we are stuck in places that have nothing to do with the Glory of God. For the purpose of this writing, the reason for being there, how long you have been there, who was right or wrong is irrelevant. God requires movement so that I will get to where Jesus is.

There are many places in Scripture where Almighty God had great destinies and momentous breakthroughs for His people but He required them to move. Abraham had to get to Mt. Moriah to sacrifice his son and then experienced the miracle of the Jehovah Jireh, God will provide. Elijah had to turn eastward to Cherith, then move to Zarephath, then go to Carmel. At Cherith he was fed by the raven, at Zarephath, he was fed by a widow, at Carmel fire fell. Moses climbed the mountain and Joshua won the battle in the valley, and the list goes on and on. There are times when God says to you that it is moving time and when you get to where I am, your breakout will be waiting for you: the enemy's counter-strategy is to keep you stuck and immovable so that you never get to the place that God has ordained.

The act of movement means that you are leaving where you are to get to where HE IS. This act is the indication to God that you are no longer willing to be stuck, immobile and intransigent. It is within your ability to make this statement and initiate this movement.

True frustration is experienced when Christians want all that God has for them but are unwilling to make a move toward God. When you do what you can, God will do what you cannot. God will never do the impossible but the realm of the impossible is accessed when you do the possible. There are so many instances all through the Word of God, when the miraculous opened to those who moved to God. Joshua is told that a great land with enormous blessing is before him but the sole of his foot must tread upon it, then it would be his. So believer, climb the mountain, scale the wall, walk through the valley and refuse to be stopped. Refuse to become stagnant, refuse to be held in the position of apathy. It is truly regrettable that so many in church life will sit without making a move toward God and their words are, "God knows where I am."

Before God sent His Son to die on the cross, in the Old Testament, God came to man. After Calvary, after God sent His Son, the people come to God. In the New Testament, Jesus says, "Come unto me, all ye that labor…". Since God gave His all and sent Heaven's best, now we give ourselves and move to Him. The breakthrough has been given, the answer has been given and the realm or sphere has been provided. It is now your time to move. The idea that people remain unmovable, and refuse to make any move to God yet they believe that God will move to them, is not scriptural. You are not waiting for God, God is waiting for you.

The prayer of John 17:24 when Jesus says to the Father that it is His will that we be with Him where He is, is a wonderful thought. The secret of success is not location, it is to get to where Jesus is. Where Jesus is, there is Glory, for the multitude followed Him into the wilderness and abundance from heaven was showered upon them. The wilderness was not a location that was wonderful in and of itself but it was miraculously transformed by the presence of Jesus.

STEP INTO THE CLOUD

Exodus 24:14-18 states: *"14 And he said unto the elders, Tarry ye here for us, until we come again unto you: and, behold,*

Aaron and Hur are with you: if any man have any matters to do, let him come unto them. ¹⁵ And Moses went up into the mount, and a cloud covered the mount.

¹⁶ And the glory of the LORD *abode upon Mount Sinai, and the cloud covered it six days: and the seventh day he called unto Moses out of the midst of the cloud. ¹⁷ And the sight of the glory of the* LORD *was like devouring fire on the top of the mount in the eyes of the children of Israel. ¹⁸ And Moses went into the midst of the cloud, and gat him up into the mount: and Moses was in the mount forty days and forty nights."*

Here is one of the Old Testament equivalents to getting to where the Almighty is. Moses told the elders that he was going to the mountain and if any matters needed to be dealt with Aaron and Hur would take care of it.

I know that there are many times when the elders of the church have much to say. This is important because elders are placed in this position to give counsel to the leader.

However, there are times when the leader must speak to the elders especially when the leader has heard from Almighty God. There are times when you must get away to the mountain of Glory to hear from Almighty God. The alternative is to be trapped in the valley dealing with matters perpetually. Moses went up into the mount and the Glory of God covered it.

Your obedience is the indication to God that you are ready to receive and walk in a supernatural realm. Moses was about to receive the law of God, the revelation from Heaven and the Glory came. Wherever the law of God is, the Glory of God is. God's Glory will never be in a place where His law, His word is not adhered to and obeyed. When you get trapped in the machinery of ministry, or you become mechanical, you are in a place of peril. Sir or madam, there must be a movement towards God. The Bible states that the Glory of God covered the mountain which begs the question, what is covering you? Even in the Holy of Holies, the Glory of God came between the wings of the Cherubim that were upon the mercy seat. One of the articles within the ark was the tablets of the law. The glory fell where the law was. You cannot separate the descent of the Glory from obedience to the word of God. Moses went up to the mountains and the cloud covered the mount. Make this move away from fleshly norms, away from usual activity, away from the mechanics of ministry, and come apart toward God on the mount. It is always an upward move.

Then an amazing comment is made. God spoke to Moses out of the cloud.

> Numbers 7:89 states: *"And when Moses was gone into the tabernacle of the congregation to speak with him, then he heard the voice of one speaking unto him from off the mercy seat that was upon the ark of testimony, from between the two cherubims: and he spake unto him."*

Moses went into the tabernacle to speak to God so he initiated the movement to the upward place. The Bible says that he heard God speaking to him from off the mercy seat from between the wings of the cherubim. God spoke to him from the appointed place which is the same as in Exodus 24:16. Where God spoke to Moses out of the cloud. But Moses would have never heard if he was not on the mountain. God will not speak to you on your terms and He will decide the place that He speaks. He is a God of order and pattern and we must make the determination to follow God's order and God's pattern. So many want to adjust the word of God to conform to their actions instead of having their actions conform to the Word of God. You will never have the mountain of Glory experience in the valley, but when the trip is made to the mountain, you can bring that mountain experience into the valley.

Now comes a revolutionary experience. Moses stepped into the midst of the cloud. What a realm to live in and experience as He stepped into the cloud. No questions were asked about success and failure, no examination of past and present. He just stepped into the cloud of glory. He went up, then he went in and there Almighty God gave him the revelation of offerings and the Ark of the Covenant. There are revelations that are released in His Glory that are not received in any other place. It seems a simple thing when people in church refuse to move and remain immobilized when the opportunity is given to move toward God. Their response is, if God is doing it at the altar, He is quite capable of doing it where I am seated. What they fail to realize, is that this is not about the capability of God, it is about your determination to leave where you are and get to where He is.

We come back to John 1:24. That says: *"Father, I will that they also, whom thou hast given me, be with me where I am; that they may behold my glory, which thou hast given me: for thou lovedst me before the foundation of the world."*

They must be where I am. It is a pride filled, arrogant, Luciferic position to remain in the place where you are and feel that God is a cosmic bell boy. The thought of these stagnated saints is that God will move on their terms. Let me give you a definition of where some people are, or an explanation of the sphere in which they live. When someone is immovable or stagnated so much that there is an indifference to spiritual movement, it is an indication of several things:

1. It indicates that a choice has been made to stay in the position that they are in.
2. It indicates that they have endorsed the continuation of the condition that they are in.
3. It indicates their refusal to submit to the Word of God.
4. It indicates the presence of self-will and it being placed above the will of God.
5. It indicates that there is a spiritual force that has held them and bound them to a life of recurring rejection.
6. It indicates that they have chosen to follow the path of flesh not the path of the Spirit. Being led by the Spirit means that you are willing to follow Him.
7. Knowing that Almighty God has much more for you and not choosing that, shows a disregard for the divine things of God.

People that choose this path of stagnation and immobility soon descend to the depths of indifference. God has given us the precious ability to choose this day whom we may serve. Let us all make the right choice.

John 17:24 talks about being where Jesus is that we may behold His glory. The translations all say, *"...we may see His glory."* It is fascinating that verse 21, says that the Glory of God given to Jesus, He gave to us. This speaks of our receiving His Glory and 2 verses down in verse 24, He speaks of beholding His Glory. Where He is, we will see or behold His Glory. When there is movement from God's people toward God, there is a movement from God towards His people. When Moses went up to the mountain, a sequence of heavenly events took place. I spoke of this before but let me repeat myself. Moses told the elders that he was going up to the mountain.

Exodus 24:12,13 states, *"12And the LORD said unto Moses, Come up to me into the mount, and be there: and I will give thee tables of stone, and a law, and commandments which I have written; that thou mayest teach them. 13And*

Moses rose up, and his minister Joshua: and Moses went up into the mount of God."

The Lord told Moses to come up and there, there God would give him the law. He then told the elders that he was going up to the mountain but Aaron and Hur would be there to take care of other matters. You must not be so involved in ministry that you forget who ministry is about. The machinery must be used by the pastor. The pastor must not be used by the machinery. Moses left the affairs of the nation in the capable hands of Aaron and Hur and he ascended to the mountain to meet with God. So do not be so trapped, surrounded, and overwhelmed by what you are doing that you cannot see whom you are doing it for. It is time to ascend to the place of revelation so that our lives can be touched by the Glory of the Almighty.

We now return to receiving His Glory that has already been given and beholding His Glory. May I submit to you that receiving this gift has to do with the inside and beholding has to do with the outside. This is Glory in two dimensions providing change, breakthrough and transformation. We have spoken of the internal enemy, the flesh, that does all it can to hinder the reception of glory. How about the enemy on the outside, the world that does all it can to create a realm of wickedness and a sphere of seduction to defeat and discourage the church of God. When I run to, come to, move toward the Lord, the next thing that happens is I behold the Glory of the Lord. I begin to see the manifestation of walking in God's realm or God's sphere. Even though I walk on the earth surrounded by all the wickedness and lust and sin, I am walking in another sphere. I am in the world, but not of the world. We must consider the idea of beholding or seeing His glory in our everyday lives, in our relationships, jobs, businesses, marriages and all that surrounds us.

Chapter 6

WALKING IN THE FLESH

"THE FLESH REALM"

The flesh as my nature, the connection with Adam, the fleshly nature inherited from Adam, is addicted to selfishness and has no other purpose but to oppose the Spirit of God. This internal enemy is at enmity with God and cannot please God. It cannot be restored nor rehabilitated and by its nature it is capable of nothing but death and destruction. Paul gives elaborate mention in Romans 6 and 7 and explains the danger of this flesh and the nature of its operation. Since the Lord has begun to give me the revelation of Glory, our meetings as I preach around the country, have ascended to another realm. Many pastors around the country can testify to this, and all Glory be to God, the word is getting around.

This in itself is the mercy of Almighty God because I am known as one of the men that have taken an unflinching stand for Israel and am able to preach intelligibly and with balance on end-time events. I have authored books on leadership, worship, the Holy Spirit, warfare and other subjects but the Prophetic message has been in great demand for many years. Since this revelation has been given to me, pastors now want a mixture of prophetic word about the coming of the Lord and the Glory of God. I said that to let you know that testimonies of deliverance by the scores have been given in these meetings. Pastors are willing to endorse this and speak of some of these testimonies. One of these testimonies came in Strafford, Missouri and I thought it was outstanding. This young lady about 27 years old, looked like her life was all together. She looked like an executive and carried herself very professionally and by looking at her you would never tell that she was suffering, and under constant attack from the enemy.

ONE NIGHT OF GLORY

One night at a Glory Conference, I spoke on stepping into the cloud where I was saying that this is not something that is future but it has already been provided. You do not have to deserve it, work for it, or fast for it, it has been given, now step into it. That night many people in Landmark Christian Center of Strafford stepped into it. This young lady was one of these people and as she came to the front she put her head on her husband's shoulder, embraced him and cried for 15 minutes. I said nothing to them and went around praying for the many that were gathered at the front of the church.

The next night she gave a stunning testimony. She said that that night she told her Lord that she must have a breakthrough, because she was at a point of giving up. For 15 years, she had to take pills to go to bed and still would not enjoy proper rest. It began to affect her entire life and she testified of the confusion, frustration and the desperation she lived in. She said that she lived in a mess, which was one of the points on my message.

The option was mess or glory. She said, she justified her mess, lived behind her mess, because then, she had no responsibility for dealing with her mess. What an astonishing insight. There are many who never get freed from the patterns of the past because they justify their mess, and live behind it. The flesh will do all it can to plead for life, and to be protected from judgment. There, hidden, covered and left alone, it wreaks havoc on lives internally and externally. When this young lady testified, it gave me an object lesson and taught me the danger of this internal flesh. She was gloriously delivered and she testified that what the enemy had tried to do in 15 years, was undone in one night. As of this writing, she is still walking in the realm or sphere of Glory. All this power, deliverance, purpose, joy and rest would have evaded her life if she were not willing to confront this flesh realm.

Here is the question, for those who will not confront the flesh realm. What are the manifestations of this flesh realm? I believe this is the first time in authoring 10 books so far, that I ever gave a testimony of someone who was delivered in one of my meetings. To that young lady I say Thank you and to that Pastor, I say Thank you for opening the door to Glory in the church you pastor.

Now let me show you how you can identify the presence of flesh and the workings of the flesh. This operation of the flesh is the hindrance to the reception of glory and the obstacle to walking in the glory. By its nature it is at enmity with God so it becomes a very dangerous enemy. It must be exposed and uncloaked so that its true nature can be seen. This is why in this chapter, I am devoting space to deal with the works of the flesh. This will not be a detailed treatment but enough to expose the presence of the flesh realm and what it produces.

THE WORKS OF THE FLESH

Galatians 5:17 states: "*For the flesh lusteth against the Spirit, and the Spirit against the flesh: and these are contrary the one to the other: so that ye cannot do the things that ye would.*"

The flesh, this sinful nature, this connection with Adam, this indication that totally leans towards self-will, self-promotion and self-absorption, wars against the Spirit of God. This flesh does not want you to be conforming to the image of God because it wants your life to reflect the dangerous liaisons of the carnal life.

Galatians 5:19-21 states: *"[19] Now the works of the flesh are manifest, which are these; Adultery, fornication, uncleanness, lasciviousness [20] Idolatry, witchcraft, hatred, variance, emulations, wrath, strife, seditions, heresies, [21] Envyings, murders, drunkenness, revellings, and such like: of the which I tell you before, as I have also told you in time past, that they which do such things shall not inherit the kingdom of God."*

This flesh has the ability to manifest itself in many forms and when these forms are lived out, the results are visible. It is impossible for someone to be dominated by flesh internally, without seeing some visible manifestation.

When Saul saved the best sheep and oxen from Amalek, he brought himself under judgment. God's instruction was that everything in Amalek must be killed but Saul saved the King and the best of the animals. What God says must be destroyed must not be saved regardless of how pleasant it seems, and how much it pleads for life. The flesh will wear any cloak to avoid detection, plead for its life when identified, to live another day to deceive, darken and destroy. When Samuel came, the sheep started to bleat and the oxen began to low. When the anointing came in the form of the prophet, the flesh was made manifest. This is why around spiritual people, carnality from others seems to be manifested. Pride wants to ascend above humility, control above submission, and selfishness above servitude.

SEXUAL SIN

The works of the flesh begin with adultery, formation and uncleanness. Adultery and fornication are running renegade in our world today leaving in its wake the shattered lives of teenagers and broken marriages. Society has so minimized the danger of these sins and so endorsed it as a social norm that children are having children.

Revelation 9:21 states:
"Neither repented they of their murders, nor of their sorceries, nor of their fornication, nor of their thefts."

Here in the tribulation period, after the Spirit of God is lifted as the hinderer to evil, fornication is one of the major evils. Adultery and fornication come from the Greek word 'porneia' and we get our English word 'pornography' from it. This too has become one of the most devastating realities, not just in the world but in church life. We have had public testimonies of deliverance from the vice like grasp of this tribulation evil. If it is not dealt with, if you hide behind the mess, then the effects will be catastrophic at every level.

The third in the line of flesh work and manifestation is uncleanness which seems to be a lethal continuation of the first two. The indication here is the thought life gone berserk descending into the deepest depth of lewdness and contamination. The thought life becomes so controlled, so oppressed that it becomes a holding place for evil. The Scripture speaks of people with an unclean spirit, and notable, is that one of them was in the synagogue. If you were to ask in the church how many have severe challenges with a reckless renegade thought life, the results might be alarming. Fornication, adultery and uncleanness are three of the poisonous evils of the flesh operation that have brought the world to the societal disaster that it is experiencing today. The evidence is: pregnant 13 year olds, teenage abortion, broken marriages and battered lives. Over 50 million babies have been killed in an abortion holocaust since Roe vs. Wade. You might ask why deal with all of this in a book on Glory. Because the presence of flesh, indulging in flesh and living in flesh are the major hindrances to the reception of and walking in the Glory of God. You must develop a disdain, a hate, a repulsion for the presence and works of the flesh. You dare not justify it or hide behind it to give it more life.

LASCIVIOUSNESS

The next work of the flesh that is mentioned is lasciviousness which is a word that is not very common to everyday usage. It is continuation of the sequence on the sexual sin and refers to renegade living and uncontrolled sexual indulgence. It seems to be the culmination of the other three that have now become uncontrolled, addictive and repetitive. Constant indulgence leads to the formation of strongholds and fortresses, so that all of life is contaminated by this evil. It must be kept in mind that deliverance is here, and another realm is here, but deliverance can only happen if this flesh is confronted. You must not justify the mess, hide behind the mess or cloak the mess.

IDOLATRY AND WITCHCRAFT

Now come idolatry and witchcraft. When we think of idolatry, we think in terms of false gods, things made of mud or stone, or reprehensible mutant looking objects as false gods. We look at bowing to these images made by the hands of men as idolatry. This is definitely an element of idolatry but I feel its deeper definition at times remains hidden.

Whatever commands your highest devotion, that is your god. When you commit your love, time, passion, pursuit to something or someone apart from the Almighty God and that thing or person is placed in the preeminent place, that constitutes idolatry. Let me give you a simple case in point. Christians pursue activities apart from work, create the time to indulge and whether it is hobbies, or activities that are enjoyed, they find the time to give to these pursuits. These things of course, in themselves are not wrong, because I myself, enjoy playing golf or going to the movies with Renee, my wife. However, some people have the passion, commitment and drive to be involved in myriad activities, yet have no time to attend a prayer meeting, or to devote to God's work. This constitutes idolatry. It is not that they do not have the time as they constantly repeat, but their choice is to pursue something else. I am always astonished that in most churches the prayer meeting has been eliminated and in others, it is very poorly attended. All this under the justification of having no time. And now who is hiding behind what? Once again this is not the book to detail these things but just to give some attention to the hindrances to Glory reception and the Glory walk.

Now comes the work of the flesh that is called witchcraft and once again we go to Revelation 9:2. It states: *"Neither repented they of their murders, nor of their sorceries, nor of their fornication, nor of their thefts."*

The Greek word for sorcerers is pharmakeia which means medicines or drugs that affect a person's personality. We get our English word 'pharmacy', so now we are linking witchcraft to drugs. So now we have the picture of addiction to prescription drugs and the presence of witchcraft. How many have become dependent on and will do anything to indulge in prescription drugs?

Now here is another aspect of this fleshly evil.

1Samuel 15:23-26 states: *"23For rebellion is as the sin of witchcraft, and stubbornness is as iniquity and idolatry. Because thou hast rejected the word of the* LORD, *he hath also rejected thee from being king. 24 And Saul said unto Samuel, I have sinned: for I have transgressed the commandment of the* LORD, *and thy words: because I feared the people, and obeyed their voice. 25 Now therefore, I pray thee, pardon my sin, and turn again with me, that I may worship the* LORD. *26 And Samuel said unto Saul, I will not return with thee: for thou hast rejected the word of the* LORD, *and the* LORD *hath rejected thee from being king over Israel."*

Rebellion is as the sin of witchcraft and it is Saul's rebellion against the word of the Lord to wipe out Amalek that caused him to lose his kingdom. Verse 23 says that stubbornness is as iniquity and idolatry. So here rebellion, witchcraft and idolatry are linked to the same verse. See how the Old Testament and the New Testament endorse each other. Witchcraft, drugs, rebellion are vitally linked to create an attack in the flesh realm. We see it – rebellion in the work place, in the home, even in the church.

THE OTHER FOUR
WORKS OF THE FLESH

These works of the flesh function in tandem and have to do with relationships. They are more readily seen and are the cause of a world of divisiveness within church life. They are probably the most visible fleshly operations within the realm of the church so they become easy to identify.

The first in this list of four is hatred. This is a word that is associated with the feeling between enemies. This word expresses great animosity, severe bitterness and unbridled hostility towards another. These refer to people who are completely opposed to each other with no desire for reconciliation. It is reprehensible, poisonous and heinous. The Scripture has much to say about hatred toward a brother but this is not a book to examine these things in detail. However we must consider the following scriptures.

1 John 2:9 states: *"He that saith he is in the light, and hateth his brother, is in darkness even until now."*

If you say you are in the light and you hate your brother then you are in darkness. It is impossible to live in light and be a hater of the brethren. You will find out in a later chapter of another book of mine on Glory, that the Glory of God lights up the entire way of New Jerusalem according to Revelation 21:23.

It is impossible to harbor hatred towards the brothers and sisters and live in the Glory sphere. Understand that before the devil can deceive and destroy, he must darken. Darkness is the work of the enemy out of which his evil is spawned.

John 2:11 states *"11 This beginning of miracles did Jesus in Cana of Galilee, and manifested forth his glory; and his disciples believed on him."*

He that hates his brother walks in darkness and does not know where he goes because the darkness has blinded his eyes. He walks aimlessly and lives in blindness. The darkness has blinded his eyes and so hatred is the work of the flesh that places people in a realm or sphere of darkness. When you did not know the Lord you lived in utter darkness but God delivered you from the power of darkness according to Colossians 1:1. Hatred is the work of the flesh that puts you back in a realm of darkness. Some try to dignify the term and call it resentment, or dislike, but again please do not justify the mess or hide behind the mess.

VARIANCE

The next work of the flesh is variance. It is the attempt to bring division by introducing your opinion and soliciting support from others to take your position. Variance does not care about the division it causes, the breakup it brings, or the bias that is introduced. It sows enormous discord and strife. As long as it gets support, any method is usable regardless of its devastating effect on others. You see this manifested in full demonic color as people criticize leadership and try to get others to be on this side of the negative destructive criticism. It creates anger and introduces a realm of viciousness that brings great hurt. At the heart of everything that brings division in the church is the force of variance.

EMULATION – WRATH

The next work of the flesh is emulation and it is translated as jealousy, or a constant desire to get the best for yourself. This is the driving force to get ahead to get what you want and if someone else gets that position, you become incensed because it was not you. The next step is to do whatever is necessary for you to achieve, regardless of the effect it has on others. Does that sound familiar in the realm of church life? This is the realm of the flesh that manifests itself with hateful force.

The next work of the flesh is wrath and it is translated as fits of rage and anger. It is the accumulation of anger on the inside that festers because of hurt or offense or disappointment because of what someone else has done. This hurt, anger, and rage are cursed and rehearsed, only waiting for the time to be explosive and destructive. So how many have nursed their hurt, their rage, their offense, their bitterness over a situation for years? How many have taken this evil, harbored it within their hearts, and are waiting for the time of manifestation?

STRIFE – SEDUCTION - HERESIES

The last three works of the flesh begin with strife. It is translated selfish ambition, a constant effort to get the best for yourself as it is rooted in selfishness. It has a connection to variance and is very obsessed with getting its own desires fulfilled. It is totally absorbed with itself and has no regard for the desires of others. It is the epitome of self-absorption and can only speak of itself. Have you ever had a conversation with someone that constantly revolves around that individual and what he or she has accomplished? They feel compelled to convey to you their excellence and their achievements. I have had the nauseating obligation to listen to the fleshly tirade of some of these that really had delusions of personal godliness. That is godliness with a very common 'g'.

Now comes the work of the flesh called seduction. It is translated dissension and factions, rebellion and defiance. It is the act of someone who refuses to submit to authority who lives as though he/she is the inherent authority and that there is no absolute authority to submit to. This person defies authority in the home, in the school, on the job, in the church. Submission to authority is never the obvious choice for in the minds of those who operate in this realm, they are superior authority. They are always more informed, more equipped and more capable. They literally live in a world of total delusory conceit.

The last work of the flesh is heresies. This word is translated factions, the feeling that everyone else is wrong except those in your little group. All these works of the flesh culminate in this evil that carries with it deviation, damnable doctrine, and deviance. It demands allegiance at the expense of everything else. Many of these heresies were dealt with in the Book of Acts and the Pauline epistles and they all were the cause of the great division and chaos in the early church.

It was never my original intention to focus in this direction in this book, but as I wrote, it became extremely clear to me that the main obstacle to receiving Glory and walking in Glory had to be dealt with. The most dangerous enemy called flesh, this unholy imposter, this cloaked hinderer must be exposed. Living in the flesh, under its power, in its realm brings death. May we never justify the mess or live behind the mess. May we never choose the path of least resistance so we absolve ourselves from the responsibility of dealing with it. May we ask the Lord for immediate discernment to know when this enemy called flesh masquerades in the religious costume and immediately amputate every connection to it!

John 1:14 states: *"And the Word was made flesh, and dwelt among us, (and we beheld his glory, the glory as of the only begotten of the Father,) full of grace and truth."*

The word became flesh and dewlt among us and we beheld His Glory, full of grace and truth. This Glory of God or truth beholding the Glory of God was actually a vital part of the life of our Lord. The disciples, the onlookers, the followers, all beheld His Glory. He really did walk in a realm, a sphere, for the Glory of God was all around Him. The idea of walking in this realm and seeing this Glory is so foreign to many Christians. It is foreign because they have been habitually walking in the wrong realm and because of this they have seen the exact opposite of Glory. After seeing this perpetually over a prolonged period, the concept of seeing the Glory of God or beholding the Glory of God becomes a far-fetched heaven later reality. This experience of Glory is postponed to the sweet by and by.

It is impossible to be where Jesus is, to have initiated spiritual movement, to have left where you are to get to where He is without seeing His Glory. When Moses stepped out of the cloud after 40 days, he had had significant internal transformation. He had heard clearly from God about building the tabernacle and the offerings that should be given to accomplish this. He had also received revelation of building the Ark of the Covenant.

After he left the mountain where he experienced the Glory of God, his priority, when he came among the people, was temple building and temple functions. He did not get wrapped up in the day to day stuff that can captivate and control. As important as day to day things are, matters related to the temple must have priority. The priority was given to building the ark, building the temple and offerings for the temple. When these things have priority, the presence of God, the Glory of God, the temple of God, then all else falls into its proper place. When other things take priority, your life is out of balance as the pursuit of things smothers the pursuit of God.

Remember, priority decides pursuit. Why are so many Christians in aggressive pursuit of material things and find themselves with a very weak and anemic commitment to God. Temple building and temple function are of little importance to so many. I am always caught by the lack of spontaneous praise in so many churches. People have to be asked, consistently pushed and prodded to give God the most elementary courtesy of a lifted hand and an open mouth. Why should something so normal to temple function elude so many. Why are some people so passionate about material life and so apathetic about spiritual development. It is fascinating in John 17:20, 26 how many times the word 'world' is used. That the world may know that the world may see. How is this going to happen? Are they going to come into the church to see this or is the church going to make His presence, His Glory visible to the world.

Remember the people of the world are only interested in seeing and hearing because they are governed by the senses. It is here that we see the enormous, external impact that is made upon a watching seeking world when we walk in and believe His Glory. When your outside begins to be transformed, they can see and know. When Moses came down from the mountain, his outer man shone so that the people could not look on His countenance. They knew that he had been with God because he came down walking in a different realm. What Moses beheld, they began to behold through him. What is the testimony that is given when the people of God live in the realm of darkness and all the world sees or beholds, is defeat, despair and devastation. Let me deal with this beholding from a prophetic perspective.

Chapter 7

PROPHETIC PERSPECTIVE ON BEHOLDING

Ezekiel 36:20-25 states that: *"**20** And when they entered unto the heathen, whither they went, they profaned my holy name, when they said to them, These are the people of the* LORD, *and are gone forth out of his land. **21** But I had pity for mine holy name, which the house of Israel had profaned among the heathen, whither they went. **22** Therefore say unto the house of Israel, thus saith the Lord* GOD; *I do not this for your sakes, O house of Israel, but for mine holy name's sake, which ye have profaned among the heathen, whither ye* *went. ²³ And I will sanctify my great name, which was profaned among the heathen, which ye have profaned in the midst of them; and the heathen shall know that I am the* LORD, *saith the Lord* GOD, *when I shall be sanctified in you before their eyes. ²⁴ For I will take you from among the heathen, and gather you out of all countries, and will bring you into your own land. ²⁵ Then will I sprinkle clean water upon you, and ye shall be clean: from all your filthiness, and from all your idols, will I cleanse you."*

The nation of Israel that was formed and called to give testimony to the word of God, found themselves in a very compromising position. The Scripture says that they profaned the name of God. The enemies of Israel asked the Israelites what they were doing in the enemies' land. Israel's enemies mocked them saying that Israel was given a land by covenant with Almighty God. Yet they were bound and battered in the enemies' land. It is here that they profaned the name of God when they began to walk in defeat, walk in other foreign heathen lands, under the control of the enemies. The testimony of walking in this realm was profanity to God and defeat to an on-looking world. This is what they were beholding everyday of their lives until He said to Israel, "I do this not for your sakes, but for mine holy name's sake." God had pity for His namesake and this is what He said, "I will take you from among the heathen I will gather you out of all countries and I will bring you into your land."

Look at the progression of His power. I will take you from among the heathen so that no power that is of the enemy will be able to dominate your life. Then I will gather you out of every country that has held you. They will not be able to hold you anymore. Then I will bring you into your land. Think about the startling difference that they were about to experience. From living in and beholding and seeing enemies, domination and control, bondage and beating, to seeing freedom, blessing, increase and inheritance. Almighty God was about to take them, gather them from all countries and bring them in. Then He said in Amos 9:13,14, 15 that no man, no power, no cartel, no nation would pluck them out of their land. Their blessing and breakthrough were about to become a reality and they were about to behold it and see it.

Ezekiel 20: 6 states: *"In the day that I lifted up mine hand unto them, to bring them forth of the land of Egypt into a land that I had espied for them, flowing with milk and honey, which is the glory of all lands."*

Israel would become THE GLORY of all lands. It was a desert, it was unproductive, it was a malarial swamp and this is what the children of Israel saw daily. I will make it glorious and they shall behold it and see it was what God now promised. The effect on the world would be profound and prophetic. What they would see would glorify Almighty God so that they would know, they would be testified to about the Glory of God. This testimony would come through Jesus and the land of Israel to the world. God has always connected His operations, His will, His purpose to the world, so that they would know. Here are some scriptures that tell you that. Ezekiel 36:23, 35,36,38. Ezekiel 38:23; Ezekiel 39:7.

To look at the land of Israel today is to behold His glory There are several vegetation zones in the world that include the Euro Siberian Zone, The Mediterranean Zone, The Inner Mongolian Zone, The Sudaneri Zone. Different food and fruit grow in these zones yet in the land of Israel there is an astonishing breakthrough. Consider the fact that 60% of Israel's land is arid desert, that in 1848 there were malarial swamps to the North and deserts to the south. Yet only in Israel do you find apples, oranges, grapes, bananas, kiwis, strawberries, watermelons growing in the same field. Nowhere in the world, even in the most fertile areas does fruit from 5 vegetation zones grow. Yet in Israel, in a desert place, a physical miracle takes place. Oh yes, she has become the glory of *ALL* lands.

There are 1500 plant species in Egypt, 1800 in the British Isles, and 3000 in Israel.

Isaiah 41:18-20 states: *"18 I will open rivers in high places, and fountains in the midst of the valleys: I will make the wilderness a pool of water, and the dry land springs of water. [19] I will plant in the wilderness the cedar, the shittah tree, and the myrtle, and the oil tree; I will set in the desert the fir tree, and the pine, and the box tree together: [20] That they may see, and know, and consider, and understand together, that the hand of the* LORD *hath done this, and the Holy One of Israel hath created it."*

In A.D. 70, the trees of Israel were viciously cut down by Titus. The Romans cut down the trees for battering rams, and for crosses. These crosses were used for the crucifixion of thousands of Christians that refused to bow to Caesar. The Muslims cut down trees to construct castles and construct castles over holy sites. The Turks cut down trees for the railroad tracks and when the Jews came back to their land, the landscape was raped and ravaged. Today the most dramatic change of terrain, possible in world history, has taken place in the land of Israel. Now there are millions of trees in the land of Israel. There are expansive forests of date palms growing in the area of the Dead Sea, Eucalyptus trees, Pignoli pines, Jerusalem pines are all in abundance. Mark Twain who came to this land in his book Innocents Abroad said, "For all lands there are for dismal scenery, I think Palestine must be prince. The hills are barren, all of color. The valleys are unsightly, deserts fringed with feeble vegetation. Every outline is harsh. It is hopelessly dreary, it is a heartbroken land."

Mr. Twain, this may have been the case in 1869 but you would love to see the dramatic, glorious transformation that has taken place. It is an exciting land, pulsating with vegetation life, outlined with oases in the desert, and a testimony to the ingenuity of a people and the covenant of God.

Isaiah 22:6 and Isaiah 62:1-4 states:

▪**22:6** *"And Elam bare the quiver with chariots of men and horsemen, and Kir uncovered the shield."*

▪**62:1-4** *"For Zion's sake will I not hold my peace, and for Jerusalem's sake I will not rest, until the righteousness thereof go forth as brightness, and the salvation* *thereof as a lamp that burneth. ² And the Gentiles shall see thy righteousness, and all kings thy glory: and thou shalt be called by a new name, which the mouth of the* LORD *shall name. ³ Thou shalt also be a crown of glory in the hand of the* LORD, *and a royal diadem in the hand of thy God. ⁴ Thou shalt no more be termed Forsaken; neither shall thy land any more be termed Desolate: but thou shalt be called Hephzibah, and thy land Beulah: for the* LORD *delighteth in thee, and thy land shall be married."*

Oh, she is flooding the world with her fruit. She is no longer desolate no longer forsaken. She is now Hepzibah or the delight of God and Beulah. God is married to the land: Scarce water, forbidding terrain, harsh soil have not stopped the transformation of this land. Today Israelis have become pioneers in agriculture. They have pioneered drip irrigation, the use of industrial waste water for agriculture, soil solarization and agricultural bio-technology. Yes a revolution has taken place in the agricultural sector in Israel that has been exposed to all parts of the world. Israel leads the world in food production per acre, fruit production per acre. She leads the world in developing strains resistant to natural hazards and special crops to withstand harsh weather. Her milk yield is the highest in the world. Consider the small population, the constant threat of neighbors and the position that the nations of the world have taken against Israel. Consider Ezekiel 37 and the valley of dry bones where its people became bleached bones that was consummated in Hitler's holocaust. And now consider the miracle of the land where the desert is blossoming like a rose, where harsh soil is commanded to sprout forth in glorious life, where with one step, you leave the Negev desert behind and step into one of the most productive pieces of land in the world. Oh Israel, people of covenant and land of covenant, oh Israel, watched over by the Almighty, oh Israel you are the glory of ALL lands.

This is what they are walking in, this is what they are now beholding every day. As of this portion that I am writing today, I am on an aircraft heading to New York to take 40 people to Israel. I will walk in the land of Glory and there behold and see the Glory of God! His land!

WALKING IN THE LAND OF GLORY

What does it mean to see God's Glory in the land of Israel? It means that there has been an utter transformation and a dramatic change since Jesus came into or moved into their land. There is the word movement again. This land has become the most productive land per capita in the world today, yet most of it is a desert. When you consider the small size of Israel, the threat leveled against her everyday, the internal conflict with Hamas and the external attack of opinion, resolutions, and forums against Israel, it is startling. Yet, in spite of this, this land is the glory of all lands. It produces more food per acre, fruit per acre than any nation in the world. It has produced the most powerful agricultural breakthroughs in the world. Visibly the land is prosperous with building going on at a record pace in the private sector and the business sector.

The first disk on key was an Israeli innovation. The ICQ instant messaging program which has become an integral part of every computer was developed in Israel. Most of the Windows XP operating system was developed in Israel. VOIP or voice over internet protocol, the basis for all programs like Skype, making international calls simple and inexpensive was developed in Israel. Israel is second place in the world after Japan and ahead of the USA in the number of patents per capita. Electronics, media supplies software, Internet security are now high on the list of not only exportable items but they are world class products. Israel has become the eighth member to join the exclusive club of nations that have successfully built and launched a satellite into orbit. Tel Aviv is the most serious competitor to Silicon Valley. The list is very, very long as to the impact that Israel has made on the entire world.

This is demographically and statistically impossible. However, the human equation is trumped by the supernatural promise. God has made this land the glory of all lands and no one can deny this. It is highly visible to an on-looking world. The Biblical idea of walking in the glory, beholding glory, and seeing glory is clearly evidenced here. The idea of having an external realm that is filled with glory is also seen here. Think of this for a moment. There are 22 nations around Israel that are antagonistic to her, some threatening to wipe her off the face of the earth. The United Nations has consistently taken a stand against the nation of Israel. The nations of the world are pressuring her to find peace by dividing her small parcel of land. Fanatical Islam has sworn to drive the Jews into the Dead, Red, Med. Sea and take Jerusalem. The numerical physical odds are against Israel. But consider this. They are in their land, per capita one of the more prosperous nations in the world, occupying their holy city Jerusalem, and she is a formidable military power. All of this after only 65 years of existence as of this writing. You hear comments like, 'This is impossible. How can this be? This cannot be true.' Oh, here is the answer, the glory of all lands. They are seeing it and beholding it and the world has a physical testimony to God's power.

THE WORLD'S RESPONSE TO THE GLORIOUS LAND

Almighty God made this prophetic statement about Israel that she would become the glory of all lands. I must pause here and give some prophetic detail to demonstrate the power of Almighty God and to show what Israelis today are beholding.

Today the attacks on Israel are myriad, coming from every possible arena. The demand of the United Nations and the nations of the world (with very few exceptions) for a two state solution, has become one of the most volatile if not the most in our world today. The nations of the world have offered a prescription for a two state solution constituting Jews and Palestinians living side by side in autonomy and peace. However, for this to happen, high pressure tactics are leveled on Israel and the major concessions, if not all are made by Israel. This is what the world is requiring from Israel:

1. Palestinian refugees must be allowed to come to Israel and settle.

2. All outposts must be destroyed.
3. All settlements must be frozen.
4. Israel must go back to its pre-1967 borders
5. Jerusalem must be divided, and become the capital of the Palestinian state.

Almighty God has made numerous prophetic statements, yet in the midst of these glorious promises, Israel is walking through the valley of international oppression. So, the fact that you are walking through a place of attack does not minimize or nullify the promises that were made. God said that they would be the glory of all lands and they would know that He is Lord. They would see His provision, power and glory and eventually they would come to their Messiah and have their ultimate Day of Atonement. I will not go into the prophetic implication of what the world wants to do with Israel because the will of God and the word of God will prevail. My emphasis is to show you that in the midst of the most violent attacks on Israel, God has the power to make Israel the glory of all lands.

Consider that when Nebuchadnezzar destroyed Jerusalem in 586 B.C., Israel never had an earthly king after this. After Titus destroyed the Temple in 70 A.D. Israel never had another Temple. Babylon took away the Kingship and Rome took the temple and the priesthood. However, it must be noted that 46 times in the Old Testament, God reiterated the oath concerning the Abrahamic covenant. The enemy could never take away the promises of God to the land and the people of Israel. Another very powerful point is in Ezekiel 36 56 times God said 'I will'. I will multiply, I will *cause*. I will sanctify, I will take, I will gather, I will bring and the list goes on.

SO THE WORLD WILL KNOW

Ezekiel 36: 35-38 states: *"35 And they shall say, This land that was desolate is become like the garden of Eden; and the waste and desolate and ruined cities are become fenced, and are inhabited. 36 Then the heathen that are left round about you shall know that I the* LORD *build the ruined places, and plant that that was desolate: I the* LORD *have spoken it, and I will do it.* ³⁷ *Thus saith the Lord* GOD; *I will yet for this be enquired of by the house of Israel, to do it for them; I will increase them with men like a flock.* ³⁸ *As the holy flock, as the flock of Jerusalem in her solemn feasts; so shall the waste cities be filled with flocks of men: and they shall know that I am the* LORD."

This land that was desolate will become like the Garden of Eden and the waste and desolate places will be fenced and will be inhabited. This is exactly what is happening in the land of Israel today. God connects these miracles to the heathen confronting the fact that He is God. You shall be the glory of all lands so the world will know that He is God. You shall be the glory of all lands so the world will know that I am the Lord. Yea, look at Gilo, Shiloh, Rishon Le'Zion, Maale Adumim, and you see wonderful, big, modern highly populated cities, bustling with activity all day. Please review some statistics to show how Israel has become the glory of all lands.

1) Israel has one fifth the population of Syria but has 10 times the economy of Syria.
2) Between 1901-2006, 750 Nobel prizes were given out, 158 were given to Jews.
3) Consider the population of about 14 million Jews world-wide and to the date of this writing, 199 Nobel prizes have been awarded to them.
4) Since its rebirth as a nation, its population has grown 10 fold and its gross domestic product has grown 50 fold.
5) Israel leads the world in developing crop strains resistant to natural hazards.
6) It has developed special crops that are resistant to harsh weather.
7) It invented drip irrigation so that water use is not wasted.
8) Since the state was established, land has increased 3 fold but agricultural output has increased 16 fold.

9) Her beehives produce per capita, more honey per hive; cows produce more milk per cow per year. She is a land flowing in Milk and Honey.

10) She has the largest desalination water plant in the world in Ashkelon.

11) She has the largest company in the world for generic medicine – Teva.

12) She leads the world in integrating nano-robotics to medicine.

13) She is the 8th member to join the exclusive club of nations who have successfully built and launched a satellite into orbit.

14) Israel's per capita income in 2000 was over $17,500.00 exceeding that of the United Kingdom.

15) Israel's 100 billion dollar economy is larger that all of its immediate Arab neighbors combined.

16) She is ranked #2 in absolute numbers of start-ups behind the USA.

17) She is the only democracy in the Middle East.

18) The cell phone was developed in Israel by Israelites working on the

Israeli branch of Motorola which has its largest development center in Israel.

19) Egypt has 1500 plant species, the British Isles have 1800, Israel has 3000.

20) Israel is the only country in the world that entered the 21st century with a net gain in its number of trees. This is astonishing considering the fact that 6000 square miles of the land of Israel is arid desert.

CONSIDER THE MIRACLE

This list could go on for another complete chapter but consider this. Consider that this country was attacked over 40 times in its history, sieged, hills leveled and valleys filled, trees rooted up by the Romans, the Turks and the Muslims. Its sacred sites were desecrated and temples torn down. Jerusalem was totally destroyed twice. Consider the population, the demographics, the constant threat around them and the attitude of the nations that surround them. Consider the implacable enemies, some of whom declare that Israel has no right to exist and that Israel spends more per capita on its own protection than any country on earth. The devil has inspired fanaticism, nations and leaders to stand in complete opposition to the land of Israel.

Yet in the midst of all of this, Almighty God has demonstrated to an on-looking world that His promises will come to pass. "I will make you the glory of all lands and you shall see and know that I am the Lord." There is a saying in Israel, 'To be a realist you have to believe in miracles.' As of this writing Israel is 65 years old and has been through 5 wars and several revolts and has won them all. You shall behold My glory is seen so vividly in the land of Israel. Logic, reason, intellect and human intelligence have no power to diffuse what has happened in this desert land.

Chapter 8

WALKING IN HIS GLORY: JUDGEMENT ON THE ENEMY

NO MORE!

Isaiah 62:1-4 states: *"¹For Zion's sake will I not hold my peace, and for Jerusalem's sake I will not rest, until the righteousness thereof go forth as brightness, and the salvation thereof as a lamp that burneth. ²And the Gentiles shall see thy righteousness, and all kings thy glory: and thou shalt be called by a new name, which the mouth of the* LORD *shall name. ³Thou shalt also be a crown of glory in the hand of the* LORD,

*and a royal diadem in the hand of thy
God. ⁴ Thou shalt no more be termed
Forsaken; neither shall thy land any more
be termed Desolate: but thou shalt be
called Hephzibah, and thy land Beulah:
for the* LORD *delighteth in thee, and thy
land shall be married."*

Verse 2 says that the Kings shall see His
Glory. It is impossible to separate this glory
from the land of Israel. Not only has God begun
to restore the people but He is restoring their
land. We know that the hearts of the Jewish
people will be turned to their Messiah but God
has also promised to touch and restore their
land. Here again are the internal and the
external. Verse 4 presents a most powerful
statement from God. You shall no longer be
termed forsaken neither shall Thy land be
termed desolate. You and your land! You shall
no longer be termed, or defined as, or
perceived as, or known as forsaken. The world
will no longer be able to call you forsaken
because a miracle is about to happen. They will
no longer, no more be able to call your land
desolate.

Then Scripture goes on to say you shall be called Hephzibah and your land Beulah. Here is the dynamic difference. The quality of your life will not be decided by what people call you because I have called you. No worldly dysfunction will stand in the way when God calls you something. You shall be called Hephzibah which means my delight. Your land shall be called Beulah, because your land shall be married. The word is NO MORE!!

When the world emblazons on its media the chaos in Israel, the people of Israel continue about their business in normalcy. I have taken groups to Israel when others have cancelled and did not have one incident. In fact, on one occasion, at midnight our people were walking in Tiberias, enjoying the peace and ambience of this beautiful spot. Yes, this is a land where you see that out of a desert, parts of it look like the Garden of Eden. In a desert you see more fruitfulness per acre than any nation in the world. At the Dead Sea you see the life of the minerals of the sea being extracted. You see, you behold and there is no physical explanation for the abundance you see in the desert. I am convinced that what is happening in that land is a promise, a guarantee of what can happen in your lives.

We too, are a people under covenant given eternal promises by Almighty God. We too serve the God of Abraham, Isaac and Jacob.

> Galatians 3:14, 29 states: *"14 That the blessing of Abraham might come on the Gentiles through Jesus Christ; that we might receive the promise of the Spirit through faith. 29 And if ye be Christ's, then are ye Abraham's seed, and heirs according to the promise."*

These verses are a guarantee that our connection to Jesus and the Abrahamic Covenant gives us the blessings of this covenant.

PROFANITY IN THE CHURCH!!

So, the thought of not choosing to be touched by His Glory, or walking in His glory, or beholding His Glory is astonishing. The result of not choosing this, is choosing another realm, another sphere and beholding and seeing the opposite every day of your life. To choose to see defeat instead of victory, weakness instead of strength, poverty instead of supply, despair instead of hope is mind blowing and it is actually demented. The spiritual parallel of Ezekiel 36 is when God's people live a life of visible defeat, complaining, bickering and the world can see no difference, the name of God is profaned. So actually, walking in the realm of mess and beholding and seeing this on a repetitive and daily basis constitutes profanity of the name of God. If you are Christian and you preach that your God is alive and His Son was raised, why are you under the control of the same things the world is controlled by? If there is no difference, who are you? When the enemy tries to keep you stuck, stagnant and seduced, it is only because he knows what it means to walk in Glory and behold and see Glory. Having a first hand, close up, throne room look at this Glory has made the enemy extremely fearful of what Glory provides. It is unthinkable, it is inconceivable that God's people would not run with desperation toward such a life and provision.

BEHOLDING AND SEEING

The beholding and seeing the Glory of God was pictured magnificently when the children of Israel followed the pillar of fire and the pillar of cloud. Once again here is the word movement. They would not move unless the cloud moved. When they did, they beheld and saw the miraculous but the world also saw the miraculous. This is a thought that many Christians never consider. When you behold, when you see, when you walk in God's Glory, the world is touched. When you choose the other fleshly, selfish, pain, the world is negatively impacted by the testimony of the fleshly life. The world is bound and fettered by fleshly operations and if the Christians are bound by the same fleshliness, what message does that send to the world? Why would they want to become Christians when some of the Christians they see are bound by the same things they are bound by? A testimony is what God has done for me, in me and through me. The John 14:20-24 prayer has assumed different dimensions for me as I see now, not only can I receive glory, but I can see Glory.

THE JERICHO OPINION

With the Ark before them or in the New Testament terms, the realm of His Glory, the children of Israel were able to walk in a realm, and behold glory on a consistent basis. Yet in spite of all of this, there was still bickering, complaining and rebelling that brought defeat to a group. However, the enemies of God had heard of His power and the testimony of the deliverance from Egypt and the victory in battle against mighty kings.

Joshua 2:9,10,11 states: *"9 And she said unto the men, I know that the* LORD *hath given you the land, and that your terror is fallen upon us, and that all the inhabitants of the land faint because of you. ¹⁰ For we have heard how the* LORD *dried up the water of the Red sea for you, when ye came out of Egypt; and what ye did unto the two kings of the Amorites, that were on the other side Jordan, Sihon and Og, whom ye utterly*

destroyed. ¹¹ And as soon as we had heard these things, our hearts did melt, neither did there remain any more courage in any man, because of you: for the LORD *your God, he is God in heaven above, and in earth beneath."*

When Joshua and Caleb came into Jericho, Rahab, an occupant of Jericho, gave testimony of what they had heard about what had happened in Egypt and the wilderness. She said that she knew that God had given them the land. A woman, living in the enemy's camp is saying I know this land is given to you by God. She follows that up by saying, "… your terror has fallen upon us." Wow! She is in this enormous fortress, surrounded by seemingly impenetrable walls, protected by kings, defended by armies and she is saying their terror had fallen on them.

People in a wilderness that are not trained warriors, have come out of bondage, walking in the realm, where they are beholding the Glory of God and now terror has fallen on enemies. So people who are in the wilderness are not necessarily of the wilderness but are seeing and beholding the glory of God in a miraculous way. Remember the Ark was before them so they were moving according to a divine pattern. I find the response of Rahab to be extremely powerful and illustrative about what the on-looking world can see and hear. Even though they were the concerted enemies of Israel, they had to recognize the sovereign God that was with them. Her first words were, "I know that the Lord hath given you." Yes, they were in the wilderness, they were not always true to their God, but as long as they followed the Ark, they saw, they beheld His Glory, provision and power which wreaked terror on marauding warriors from the wilderness group. This rally is a testimony to the magnificence of our Lord.

But her commentary continues in Joshua 2:11 when she said, "As soon as we had heard these things our hearts did melt." Isn't this an amazing thing? The heart of the enemy melts because of what they have heard about the God of the wilderness travelers. We have heard of what your God is doing for you and our heart has melted. The next few words add to the demise of the enemy when she says, "Neither did there remain any more courage in any man…." The heart melts and now the courage is gone so we know that when you arrive at Jericho, inevitable defeat is before us. This is actually seen in Joshua 6:1, 2. Jericho, this imposing, enormous, walled stronghold was shut up, and no one came out and no one went in and it was shut up because of God's people. Can you imagine that the greatest stronghold or fortress of the Canaanites, is shut up because of the wilderness journey men and women? Would to God that Christians today could find the power of following the Ark, walking in His Glory. Why is it so easy for us to study this wilderness journey, see the Ark, the pillar of fire and the pillar of cloud and not understand?

We teach and preach about all the manifestations failing to realize none of this is possible without following the Ark. Yes, you can walk in His Glory, they did. Yes, you can behold His Glory, they did. Yes, you can show the on-looking world that your God is above all, they did. All this from the desert circumstance of the wilderness.

Ezekiel 36:23 rings out as it says, *"I will be sanctified in you, before their eyes."*

This work will be done to you, in you, through you and around you. Let it not be easy for you to quote what happened to them and not see the possibility of that happening to you.

Walking in God's realm, beholding and seeing God's Glory has nothing to do with the presence of the world's system, spirit, or the worldly place that surrounds you. My life is not framed by the things that are around me but by the Almighty God who is above me and in me. There are times when I have spoken in private settings about the Glory of God and the response of some has been, wait I have to process this. The thought of Christians walking in the realm of Glory while on earth should be readily accepted but many find it hard to accept. I submit that the main reason is that for so long many have been walking in an oppressed, targeted, attacked, weakened realm so that any other walk is foreign.

Add to that, the walk of Glory, or seeing His Glory and it all becomes more complex. If you ask the question, "What are you beholding or what are you seeing?", the answer would be very revealing. Here the children of Israel were delivered from bondage like we are; they were walking through a wilderness like many are, yet they saw His Glory, like we should. We accept the deliverance, agree with walking in the wilderness but have to process the thought of walking in and seeing the Glory. May processing end today and the beholding begin in glorious fashion.

CONCLUSION

This glorious prayer of John 17:20-26 assumes eternal significance for our lives as hopefully we now begin to understand to some degree, the enormity of this prayer. The prayer that speaks of His Glory given must now be received. The continuation of this prayer that says that they may behold My Glory lets us know that it is His will for Glory to be around us. If the world can surround people with trauma, trial, and turmoil, doesn't God who is infinitely more powerful, have the ability to affect what is around me? Yes, He is able to change what is in me but I know He is also able to change what is around me. This affects how I walk, in what realm I walk, and what I behold.

The very life of Christ on earth is the greatest illustration of walking in the glory or walking in God's Glory realm. Even though there were times when he was in adverse circumstances or criticized, or mocked, He was able to walk in the realm of God's power and glory.

In a storm, He sleeps and then stills the wind. In a desert, He multiplies the bread and fish. On a cross He opens heaven for a dying thief. His birth, His life, His death, His resurrection were all in a realm of Glory. I hope by now you can see that this internal and external Glory have already been given. I hope that you will be able to say, this is what I want and this is the way I choose to live. I am a temple created and fashioned to house the Glory of Almighty God. I will no longer be stagnated, or immobile. I will move towards my Lord and behold His Glory. I will no longer be beaten and buffeted by oppressive surroundings because even though I may be in a wilderness, I will walk in His realm of Glory. It is not based on what I have done but because of what Jesus has done. It is not because of what I have been though but because of what He went through. In this prayer, God gave this Glory to Jesus and Jesus gave this Glory to us. What a glorious sequence of transmissions from the Almighty God to Jesus to us.

I myself have been deeply affected by the revelation of Glory. I am on my way to Israel and even though I have been there many times, I look forward to this trip with eager anticipation. I will see His Glory in greater fashion. May the Glory of Almighty God abound in you and around you as we journey together on this wonderful path.

ABOUT SHERLOCK BALLY

Sherlock Bally has been an ordained minister for thirty-five years. He attended Southern Bible College in Houston, Texas and did post graduate studies at Luther Rice Seminary and International Bible Seminary. After attending college, Sherlock went to Trinidad, where he was born and pastored the church where he was saved. For fourteen years in Trinidad his duties included the pastorate of a growing church, a nationally televised program and a radio ministry reaching most of the Caribbean.

He was held hostage by fanatical Islamic adherents in 1990 and was miraculously delivered. His call to the nations led to a move back to the United States and from 1990 to 2007 he has made 62 overseas trips in crusades and conventions. He has appeared on the Trinity Broadcasting Network on several occasions, and makes several television and radio appearances. He has ministered with Hal Lindsey, Jack Van Impe, Grant Jeffrey, Perry Stone and many others. God has gifted Sherlock in the revelation of end-time prophecy and the subsequent application of prophetic truth to personal life. His passion is to see the lost saved, the saved sent and the sent empowered. He understands the primacy of the local church and the paramount position of the pastor in these days of harvest. He believes that this is the season of reclamation, restoration, and restitution.

Sherlock carries a powerful evangelistic anointing and thousands are saved in this country every year in his meetings. He is anointed to identify the attack of the enemy in everyday situations and arm believers with weapons of faith to win in the combat zone.

In 2006, Sherlock was appointed by the Christian Allies Caucus of the Knesset as their liaison to the pastors of North America. The Knesset is the government of Israel. The Christian Allies Caucus is comprised of fifteen members of Israel's government. Their purpose is to bring Israel and the Christians closer together. Sherlock sees this Judeo-

Christian alliance as pivotal and an integral part and a vital component to Gods Timeline. Recently Dr. Bally was also named by the Christian Allies Caucus to be the Executive Director of the Caribbean Israel Allies Foundation. This foundation is dedicated to all the Islands of the Caribbean in order to bring all the people of the Caribbean in closer relationship to the Knesset.

He has authored over seven books and believes in the vital educational aspect of ministry. He is married to Renee' his wife of 32 years and is the father of Rachel and Micah.